Cooking for Your Man

Cooking for Your Man

Yolanda Banks
and Melissa Clark

Broadway Books / New York

PUBLISHED BY BROADWAY BOOKS

Published in the United States by Broadway Books,
an imprint of The Doubleday Broadway Publishing Group,
a division of Random House, Inc., New York.

www.broadwaybooks.com

BROADWAY BOOKS and its logo, a letter B bisected on the
diagonal, are trademarks of Random House, Inc.

Book design by Barbara Balch

Library of Congress Cataloging-in-Publication Data
Banks, Yolanda, 1974–
Cooking for your man / Yolanda Banks and Melissa Clark.
p. cm.
ISBN-13: 978-0-7679-2192-3
ISBN-10: 0-7679-2192-5
1. Cookery. I. Clark, Melissa. II. Title.
TX714.B35 2006
641.5—dc22
2006042583

PRINTED IN THE UNITED STATES OF AMERICA

10 9 8 7 6 5 4 3 2 1

First Edition

This book is dedicated to my wonderful, loving, supportive husband, Tony, who has believed in me from the very beginning, and whom I love dearly. He is the inspiration for and the spirit behind this book.

Contents

Acknowledgments

Like a successful marriage and a winning football team, producing a cookbook is a group effort. There are many people who helped make this book a reality, and I am happy to have the chance to thank them.

But first and above all, I must thank my Lord and Savior Jesus Christ for giving me the talent and passion for food, and the hope and patience to pursue my dreams.

Then, there is, of course, my family, the Warrs, because without them I probably wouldn't have developed a love for food in the first place. They taught me a lot over the years, and I am very grateful for all those lessons and amazing meals!

Not only did my brother Levon push me to write this book in the first place, he also made it possible by helping me get all my recipes into the computer—no small job.

Many thanks to Paul Fedorko, my agent, who believed in my vision and found it a home at Broadway Books. And to my editor there, Jennifer Josephy, who gave me such excellent direction and helped shape the book in countless ways.

Thanks, too, to my coauthor, Melissa Clark, who helped me put my stories and thoughts on paper. Melissa was a sheer joy to work with; her verve and talent really set her apart. And to her team, Karen Rush, Melissa Vaughan, Zoe Singer, and Sarah Huck, for recipe testing and editing help.

Photographer Dana Gallagher and her team of stylists made my recipes look mouth-wateringly delicious.

And of course, to Tony, my husband, for everything, always.

Cooking for Your Man

Introduction

If you could go back in time to when I was a skinny, spaghetti-loving ten-year-old growing up in East Lansing, Michigan, and tell my family I would be a cookbook author, nobody would be surprised. But if you could go back to just before I met my husband, quarterback Tony Banks, when he was playing for Michigan State, and tell him he'd be eating sashimi and foie gras like they were going out of style, he would say, "Oh, no, I'm not eating that!" Tony grew up on Spam and sports, whereas I was hanging around my grandmother in the kitchen even before I was tall enough to see above the counter. But now we love eating together, whether we're trying a new restaurant or eating dinner in. Over the course of our relationship I've developed a collection of recipes we turn to again and again. These recipes are the basis of this book, *Cooking for Your Man,* dedicated to Tony, of course.

Don't take the title too literally. For me, eating with and cooking for the people you care about is one of the most important things that you can share with others— whether it's your man, woman, child, partner, devoted friend, parent, or sibling. There really is no better way to show people you love them than to cook them something you know they'll adore, whether it's a quick batch of Chocolate Waffles (page 155) or a more special, fancier treat, like my spicy Cajun Seafood Pasta (page 71). I love feeding people and knowing they are being nurtured and nourished, and, while I can and often do get a satisfying dinner on the table in no time, I'm also happy standing in the kitchen for hours to make a blow-out meal. I come from a food-focused family, so I grew up around cooks, and cooking was an integral part of our birthdays, holidays—any reason to celebrate. And when I say food, I mean all kinds of food, and lots of it.

My grandmother Jacqueline has traveled all over the world, and her cooking techniques borrow something from every place she's been. For example, when she came back from France, she began making coq au vin. We didn't eat a typical Midwestern diet. For one thing, we never used bottled pasta sauces or mixes of any kind. Everything we ate was made from scratch, which is particularly impressive when you consider that my mom was a single working mom for most of my brother Levon's and my childhood. And while we didn't think about seeking out fresh herbs and getting the best fresh ingredients the way I do now, my grandmother had a garden full of cabbages, corn, tomatoes, and greens, so we were enjoying fresh, healthy foods without thinking about it.

I was the first grandchild on that side of the family, and ever since I can remember I was always picking vegetables in the garden, and I was always the one in the kitchen saying, "I wanna help do this, I wanna help do that." I remember being so excited about the food my grandmother made for my aunt's high school graduation. There were ham roll-ups, and a watermelon boat filled with perfectly round melon balls. I even made pasta from scratch when I was ten, and as I got more into cooking, my grandmother was happy to step aside and let me take over. I always used to help her on Thanksgiving, and I'd get there before my aunts did. When I was in high school I asked if I could make Thanksgiving dinner, and, aside from the turkey and dressing, which no one makes better than Gran, I cooked every dish.

Birthdays were highlight meals. In my mom's family, when it's your birthday, you choose the menu. I always chose spaghetti, garlic bread, and pineapple salad. Levon, on the other hand, used to ask for crab legs—and crab legs for fifteen people is a real splurge! But I just wanted spaghetti. Back then my tastes were simple. I still love spaghetti, although now I'm more likely to make my own fresh pasta and just toss it with some tomatoes, garlic, and fresh herbs simmered in a little olive oil, so that the flavor of the pasta shines. But back then it would be Gran's meat sauce, and even as a skinny eight-year-old I would have the biggest plate of everybody, including the men. They would all say, "Your eyes are too big for your stomach," "You're never going to finish all that," and I'd always finish it, every bite.

Every birthday would end with one of my granddaddy's layer cakes. Since my mom and I have the same birthday, and we both love lemon, he'd make a vanilla layer cake with a little lemon juice in the batter, and then he'd make a lemon frosting. Granddaddy and my aunt Toni are the bakers in the family. I remember that when my aunt Toni was still in college, my brother and I would go to her house and she'd make pizza from scratch, with homemade dough and a pizza stone—the whole bit. Later she opened a muffin business called Little Miss Muffin. She made more than fifty different kinds of muffins, including a bacon, Cheddar, and egg muffin, which was like a little meal in itself, and Hawaiian muffins with pineapple and macadamia nuts, which I've included here. Her muffins are very, very light, and that makes it easy to eat more than one at a time. She and I collaborated on making the perfect apple pie, getting the crust just right. And we've had countless New York–style cheesecake trials to come up with one just the way we like it.

Really everyone in the family is a great cook in his or her own right. Everyday meals were always great when I was growing up, too, and that's something I believe in—delicious food for special occasions, and for no occasion other than that you love the person you're cooking for. My mom's fried chicken and amazing macaroni and cheese were every-day foods that were incredibly good. All the cousins back in Michigan miss those dishes now that she's moved to Dallas—no one else makes them the same. And Gran's dishes were all so simply delicious, whether it was her rump roast or her baked chicken. Those dishes sound pretty plain, but when you season the meat really well and take the care to baste it, it's so flavorful and juicy.

I was always right there in the kitchen learning whenever any cooking was going on, and I've been in the kitchen ever since. I was the cheerleader who all the other cheer-leaders wanted to make the Jell-O shots, and in high school I would bake brownies and cookies for friends. In college in Atlanta I was friends with the guys across the street, and whenever they had a girl over, they wanted me to cook a whole meal and pretend that they did it—and I would!

I cooked through college, gathering recipes all the way. When a friend of my mom's who was working in Greece needed someone to help, I volunteered, and I fell in love with that cuisine. I loved the markets and the fresh fish. I still could eat fish every day, although Tony needs to have a steak every now and again. In Greece I never knew what fish I was buying, but I knew how to buy a fresh one, and cook it well, and they were all so wonderful. I make a Greek yogurt dish called Tzatziki (page 11), with cucumbers and garlic, and Tony loves it. The dishes I cook for Tony come from everywhere I've been, whether it's Spinach Salmon Spring Rolls (page 22), from a restaurant he and I used to go to a lot, Spiced Basmati Rice Pilaf (page 147), or Gran's Beef Stroganoff (page 113). It's all just good, satisfying food with a lot of flavor and texture, because if I'm cooking for Tony it's got to have crunch. And for weeknight dinners, my recipes are pretty simple. They taste great because they're based on good flavors and the best ingredients.

Of course I also do it up sometimes, and make something like Beef Wellington with Cabrales (page 122), which is very involved. You sear the meat, sauté portobellos, and add Cabrales, which is Tony's favorite blue cheese, then bake it under pastry with caramelized onions. I served that recipe with Lobster Mashed Potatoes (page 144) for Tony one special night, and he said, "We need to have this once a week." I said, "Honey, people don't eat beef Wellington once a week; they eat it once a year. It's a special-occasion dish, and it's so heavy!" But he just loves it, so I will make it from time to time, like if we have a few of Tony's teammates over for a quarterback dinner.

But *Cooking for Your Man* isn't about big, rich dishes all the time. We eat more healthfully now than we used to. When we were in college we really used to eat some junk. And back then, Tony used to challenge me to eating contests and I would do it, because even though I've always been slim and he's a 230-pound football player, I can eat more than he does.

Luckily, I'm very active, and when I'm not playing tennis or walking the dog I'm working out, so I don't put on weight. I've always been into sports and I love to be moving. And while Tony is a big guy, he's actually a pretty lean football player, as they come. Most of our meals are based on fresh, healthy ingredients—things you can eat even if you don't play football! And now that I'm finally putting recipes into a cookbook, it's important to me to reflect that balance. My recipes are not restaurant food, or TV test-kitchen food; they're the actual meals I've been making over the years, and they're a well-balanced, eclectic mix.

Even though I've been cooking for most of my life, until five years ago it hadn't occurred to me that I could turn my passion for food and for teaching other people to cook into a career. But I managed to do plenty of cooking and teaching anyway.

Four years ago, I talked a friend who doesn't eat red meat through a steak dinner she wanted to cook for her boyfriend's birthday, and she claims that he still talks about that meal to this day. She didn't even have a good pan or grill, so I told her to get a cast-iron skillet. Then we spent two hours on the phone while I explained how to heat and season the pan with oil, put plenty of salt and freshly ground pepper on the steak, and make a roasted-red-pepper sauce, asparagus bundles tied with scallions, and roasted-garlic mashed potatoes. It's the kind of meal that everyone should have up their sleeve for a night when they want to make a splash.

So my goal in this book is to show how a real person at home can make meals that are inspiring and satisfying without a lot of fancy gadgets and weird ingredients. Just like when I describe how to make good gumbo to my girlfriends over the phone, here I'm trying to give cooks confidence to try something that may be new but is totally accessible. You can be sure that when you make one of these dishes for your loved ones, it will turn out as beautifully and deliciously as it does for mine.

Appetizers
and Nibbles

Perfect Spicy Guacamole

1 garlic clove, minced

1/4 cup chopped red onion

2 tablespoons chopped fresh cilantro

2 teaspoons chopped jalapeño pepper

1 teaspoon kosher salt

3 tablespoons chopped fresh tomato

1 tablespoon freshly squeezed lime juice

2 Hass avocados, pitted and chopped

Who doesn't love guacamole? Me, for one. But that was a long time ago. I used to hate it, because the avocados were always too ripe and mushy. I had been making it for my man for years and then finally something clicked—use ripe but firm avocados, which mash up into small chunks but don't turn into a runny puree. I like to use a *molcajete*, a Mexican mortar and pestle, to keep it really authentic. It may seem like you're adding a lot of salt, but avocados need plenty to bring out their flavor. I like guacamole on the spicy side, so I leave the seeds in the jalapeño. If you prefer it mild, seed the pepper before chopping it. **Makes 4 servings**

1. In a small bowl using the back of a wooden spoon, or in a molcajete, mash together the garlic, 1 tablespoon of the red onion, 1 teaspoon of the cilantro, 1 teaspoon of the jalapeño, and the salt until the mixture forms a wet paste.

2. Add the remaining onion, cilantro, and jalapeño, and the tomato, lime juice, and avocados, and mix well. Taste and adjust the seasoning if necessary. Serve with tortilla chips.

Gold Coast Margaritas

Makes 4 servings

What makes this margarita so special is the mix from Williams-Sonoma, in which Meyer lemons and Key limes are combined to make it a real treat. The Meyer lemons give it a slight sweetness, and the Key limes give it a kick.

1. Rub a lime wedge around the rims of 4 margarita or cocktail glasses, then dip the rims into a saucer filled with coarse salt. Fill the glasses with ice.

2. Fill a large cocktail shaker halfway with ice. Add the tequila, margarita mix, Cointreau, and both lime juices. Cover and shake for 30 seconds.

3. Strain the mixture into the prepared glasses. Float 1 teaspoon of Grand Marnier in each glass and garnish with lime wedges.

1 lime, cut into wedges

Coarse salt

8 ounces premium tequila (such as Herradura Silver)

8 ounces Williams-Sonoma margarita mix

4 ounces Cointreau

1 ounce Rose's lime juice

Freshly squeezed juice of 1 lime

4 teaspoons Grand Marnier

Creamy Hummus

For the baked pita chips:
4 (6-inch) whole wheat pitas
4 (6-inch) pitas
Olive oil spray
Kosher salt

2 cups canned chickpeas,
  rinsed and drained
2/3 cup tahini (sesame paste)
2 tablespoons roasted garlic
  paste (see box)
Freshly squeezed juice of
  1/2 lemon
2 tablespoons roughly
  chopped fresh flat-leaf
  parsley
1 tablespoon ground cumin,
  toasted
1/4 teaspoon kosher salt, plus
  additional to taste
1/4 teaspoon freshly ground
  black pepper
1/2 cup low-sodium chicken
  broth or stock
1 1/2 tablespoons extra virgin
  olive oil

Hummus is a tasty and healthy snack when you serve it with baked pita chips or cut-up veggies for dipping. It's also great as a spread on sandwiches or wraps. This is a particularly creamy but low-fat version. By using chicken broth in place of much of the oil, I've cut calories without losing any flavor. **Makes 8 servings**

1. To make the pita chips, preheat the oven to 350° F. Slice the pitas in half horizontally and spray each side with olive oil. Stack the pitas and cut into sixths to make chips. Place the chips in a single layer on 2 baking sheets and season generously with salt. Bake 6 to 8 minutes, until lightly browned and crisp. The chips will keep for two days, stored in an airtight container.

2. In a food processor fitted with the blade attachment, combine the chickpeas, tahini, garlic paste, lemon juice, parsley, cumin, salt, and pepper, and process until well combined. Add the chicken broth and 1 tablespoon of the olive oil and process until smooth. Taste and adjust the seasoning if necessary.

3. Spoon the hummus into a serving bowl and drizzle with the remaining ½ tablespoon of olive oil.

Roasted Garlic Paste

To make the roasted garlic paste, preheat the oven to 400° F. With a sharp knife, remove the top third of a head of garlic and drizzle with 2 teaspoons of extra virgin olive oil. Wrap in a square of aluminum foil and roast about 45 minutes, until very soft and golden. Let cool, then squeeze out the garlic.

Tzatziki
(Greek Yogurt Dip
with Garlic and Cucumbers)

Years ago, I spent several weeks in Greece working for a friend of my aunt Toni. That's where I fell in love with this mealtime staple. If you can find Greek yogurt, use it. It's thicker than the usual plain yogurt, and even the low-fat kind is supercreamy. Just make sure not to use fat-free yogurt—there's way too much water in it. **Makes 8 servings**

1. Place the chopped cucumber in a sieve and sprinkle it with the salt, tossing well to mix. Set the sieve over a bowl, cover tightly with plastic wrap, and drain for 3 hours at room temperature. Line another sieve with cheesecloth and place the yogurt on top of the cloth. Place the sieve over a bowl, cover tightly with plastic wrap, and drain for 3 hours at room temperature.

2. Once the cucumber and yogurt have released all of their liquid, transfer them to a medium bowl. Add the garlic, mint, lemon juice, olive oil, oregano, salt, and pepper. Stir gently to combine. Taste and adjust the seasoning if necessary. The tzatziki can be stored in an airtight container in the refrigerator for up to 2 days. Serve at room temperature, with warm pita bread or baked or grilled pita chips (see page 10) for dipping.

1 large English cucumber, peeled and roughly chopped

1 teaspoon kosher salt

2 1/2 cups plain low-fat or whole-milk yogurt

5 garlic cloves, minced

1/4 cup finely chopped fresh mint leaves

Freshly squeezed juice of 1 lemon

1 tablespoon extra virgin olive oil

1/2 teaspoon dried oregano

Kosher salt and freshly ground black pepper

Pita bread

Hot Artichoke Spinach Dip

For the baked tortilla chips:

Olive oil spray

4 (6- to 8-inch) corn tortillas

4 (6- to 8-inch) sun-dried-tomato tortillas

4 (6- to 8-inch) cilantro-flavored tortillas

Kosher salt

4 tablespoons (1/2 stick) unsalted butter

1/4 cup all-purpose flour

1/2 cup finely chopped shallots

1 tablespoon minced garlic

2 cups whole milk

1/4 teaspoon freshly grated nutmeg

1/2 teaspoon kosher salt

1/4 teaspoon freshly ground black pepper

1/2 cup grated Fontina cheese

1/4 cup grated Parmigiano-Reggiano cheese

1 (10-ounce) package frozen chopped spinach, thawed and drained

2 (14-ounce) cans artichoke hearts, drained and chopped

My take on this classic hot dip has more verve than most recipes, since I've dressed it up with Fontina and Parmigiano-Reggiano cheeses. I always try to serve it with homemade chips, which I make from assorted tortillas—corn, sun-dried tomato, and cilantro. It really kicks up the flavor.

Makes 8 servings

1. To make the tortilla chips, preheat the oven to 350° F. Spray both sides of the tortillas with the olive oil spray. Stack the tortillas and cut them into sixths to make the chips. Spread the chips in a single layer on 2 large baking sheets and season them generously with salt. Bake 10 to 15 minutes, until crisp. The chips can be made up to 2 days ahead, cooled, and stored in an airtight container.

2. Preheat the oven to 400° F. In a medium saucepan over medium heat, melt the butter. Whisk in the flour, stirring constantly, until the roux is light brown, about 5 minutes. Add the shallot and garlic and sauté until soft, about 2 minutes.

3. Whisk in the milk and bring to a boil. Season with the nutmeg, salt, and pepper. Simmer, uncovered, until the sauce coats the back of a spoon, about 5 minutes. Remove from the heat and stir in both cheeses.

4. Using a clean kitchen towel, squeeze the excess water from the spinach, then add it to the cheese mixture along with the artichoke hearts, stirring to combine. Taste and adjust the seasoning if necessary.

5. Place the cheese mixture in a baking pan or gratin dish and bake 10 to 15 minutes, until golden brown. Serve it with the baked tortilla chips.

Crazy Hot Crab Dip

I love crabmeat, and this dip just shines with it. Jumbo lump crab is the best kind to use here because it comes in nice, meaty chunks; but you can use any kind of crab, as long as you buy it in a container from a fishmonger. Canned crab has a very mushy texture, which, unlike the lump crab, can disappear in the dip. I think this is a great dip to serve with cocktails, like a nice, chilly, sweet, and tart Appletini (see box). **Makes 8 servings**

1. Preheat the oven to 350° F. In a medium bowl, combine the Miracle Whip, cilantro, chipotle, lime juice, garlic paste, and Worcestershire sauce, and mix well. Stir in the cheeses until well incorporated.

2. Gently fold in the crabmeat, making sure not to break up the lumps. Pour the mixture into a baking pan or gratin dish and bake about 20 minutes, until golden brown and bubbling. Remove the dip from the oven and let cool for about 5 minutes before serving. Serve with pita chips.

2/3 cup Miracle Whip light or mayonnaise

1/4 cup finely chopped fresh cilantro

1 tablespoon minced chipotle pepper (see page 35)

1 tablespoon freshly squeezed lime juice

2 teaspoons roasted garlic paste (see box, page 10)

1 teaspoon Worcestershire sauce

1/3 cup grated sharp white Cheddar cheese

1/3 cup grated Monterey Jack cheese

1 pound jumbo lump crabmeat, picked clean

Pita chips (see page 10, or store-bought)

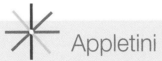

Appletini

Makes 2 servings

4 ounces premium vodka (such as Belvedere)

5 ounces pineapple juice

3 ounces sour apple Pucker schnapps

1 Granny Smith apple, sliced, optional

1. Fill a shaker halfway with ice. Add the vodka, pineapple juice, and schnapps. Cover and shake well for 1 minute.

2. Strain into chilled martini glasses and top with apple slices, if using. Serve immediately.

Jamaican Jerk Chicken Wings

1 tablespoon whole allspice

1 teaspoon whole cloves

1 cinnamon stick

1 cup chopped scallions

1/4 cup soy sauce

1/4 cup freshly squeezed lime juice

2 Scotch bonnet or serrano chile peppers, seeded and minced

2 tablespoons dark rum (preferably Appleton from Jamaica)

2 tablespoons canola oil

1 tablespoon dried thyme

1 tablespoon light brown sugar

1 tablespoon kosher salt

1 tablespoon minced garlic

1 tablespoon freshly grated ginger

1 1/2 teaspoons freshly grated nutmeg

3 pounds chicken wings (see note)

Cooking spray

Whenever I vacation in Jamaica, I always make sure to eat jerk chicken. It's one of my favorite dishes. This recipe takes me right back to the Jamaican beach. It's not too spicy, but it's full of flavor. If you have time, marinate the wings a day ahead. They taste better that way because they really have a chance to absorb all those amazing seasonings. The jerk mix also works well on salmon. Pair it with a piña colada and you'll definitely think you're on vacation. **Makes 6 servings**

1. In a small dry skillet over medium heat, place the allspice, cloves, and cinnamon. Toast the spices, stirring constantly, until fragrant, about 3 minutes. Let cool, then transfer to a spice grinder and finely grind.

2. In a food processor or blender, combine the ground spices, scallions, soy sauce, lime juice, chiles, rum, oil, thyme, sugar, salt, garlic, ginger, and nutmeg, and process until smooth. Taste and adjust the seasoning if necessary.

3. In a large dish, arrange the wings in a single layer and pour the marinade over them, stirring to coat. Cover the wings tightly with plastic wrap and marinate in the refrigerator for at least 2 hours, preferably overnight.

4. Preheat the oven to 450° F. Cover a broiling pan with foil and coat it with cooking spray. Arrange the wings in a single layer on the pan. Spoon the excess marinade on top. Bake the wings in the upper third of the oven 30 to 40 minutes, until cooked through.

Note: Removing Wing Tips To remove the wing tip, use a sharp knife to cut the chicken wing between the first and second joint. The wing tips can be discarded or saved for use in soup or stock.

Piña Colada

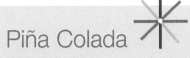

Makes 4 servings

There are two variations of this drink. The first is a nonalcoholic version in which you simply omit the rum. The second version is known on the islands as a Lava Flow. This is my favorite drink to have by the beach. Make the piña colada as directed. In a blender, puree one 10-ounce package of frozen sweetened strawberries. Coat each glass with 1 to 2 ounces of strawberry puree. Pour in the blended colada. Using a spoon, drag the puree up through the colada, creating a stripe. Serve as directed.

In a blender, combine all the ingredients except the pineapple wedges. Blend until smooth, pour into cocktail glasses, and garnish with pineapple wedges.

2 cups crushed ice

1 1/2 cups pineapple juice

3/4 cup Coco Lopez coconut cream

6 ounces light rum (such as Bacardi)

2 ounces dark rum (Captain Morgan's)

4 pineapple wedges

Aunt Laura's Teriyaki Wings

When there's a big game, my aunt Laura's teriyaki wings always make an appearance. They are so yummy and tender—with a salty, sweet, and tangy taste that I love. The teriyaki marinade is also excellent on chicken legs and thighs, and you can cook them the exact same way, adding on a few minutes at the end if they aren't quite done. **Makes 6 servings**

1 cup low-sodium chicken broth or stock

1 cup low-sodium soy sauce

1/2 cup dark brown sugar, packed

1/4 cup chopped scallions

Freshly squeezed juice of 2 limes

4 garlic cloves, minced

3 pounds chicken wings, wing tips removed (see note, page 14)

1. In a large bowl, combine the chicken broth, soy sauce, brown sugar, scallions, lime juice, and garlic, and mix well. Place the chicken wings in a nonreactive bowl and pour the marinade over the wings. Cover tightly with plastic wrap and refrigerate overnight.

2. Preheat the oven to 450° F. Using a slotted spoon, transfer the chicken wings to a large baking dish and bake, covered, for 20 minutes. Uncover the dish and continue to bake another 20 minutes, or until very tender. Serve immediately.

Chicken Quesadillas with Mango

8 (8-inch) flour tortillas

1 whole roasted chicken, skinned and boned

2 mangoes, peeled and sliced

1 small shallot, thinly sliced

1/4 cup chopped fresh cilantro

1 cup shredded Havarti cheese

Canola oil, for brushing

Pico de gallo or mango relish (see box)

These quesadillas can be whipped up and brought to the table in minutes. The trick is to buy a preroasted chicken. You can substitute any cheese, but I think the combination of Havarti and mango is magical. **Makes 8 servings**

1. Preheat the oven to 450° F. To assemble the quesadillas, line 2 baking sheets with parchment paper or foil and place 2 tortillas on each. Divide the chicken, mango, shallot, and cilantro among the tortillas and top with the cheese and the remaining tortillas, pressing gently on each quesadilla so it all sticks together when you bake it.

2. Brush the tops of the quesadillas with canola oil. Bake 6 to 8 minutes, until lightly browned and slightly crisp. Cut them into quarters and serve, topped with pico de gallo or mango relish.

Pico de Gallo

Pico de gallo, literally "rooster's beak" in Spanish, is a Mexican relish made from chopped tomatoes, red onion, hot peppers, lime juice, and cilantro. To make a sweet and spicy version, mango can be substituted for the tomato. Both pico de gallo and mango relish are also available at specialty food stores or in the ethnic-foods section of the supermarket.

✳ Buffalo Chicken Tenders

Tony loves buffalo chicken wings, but I prefer buffalo tenders, made from white-meat chicken breasts. This recipe doesn't have a crunchy coating, but the chicken gets nice and crusty from the high heat in the oven. Don't be tempted to skip the blue cheese dressing—it rocks. **Makes 6 servings**

1. Preheat the oven to 400° F. Season the chicken with the seasoned salt, garlic powder, and black pepper, and set aside. In a large bowl, whisk together the melted butter and hot sauce until combined. Reserve a third of the mixture and set aside.

2. Toss the chicken strips with the remaining sauce to coat. Place the chicken on a foil-lined baking sheet and cook in the lower third of the oven, turning once, 5 to 6 minutes per side, until the juices run clear. Remove the chicken from the oven and toss with the reserved sauce.

3. To make the blue cheese dressing, in a small bowl combine the blue cheese, sour cream, Miracle Whip, lemon juice, Worcestershire sauce, honey, cayenne, and salt, and mix well. Taste and adjust the seasoning if necessary.

4. Serve the chicken tenders hot, with celery and carrot sticks and the blue cheese dressing on the side for dipping.

For the chicken tenders:

3 pounds boneless, skinless chicken breasts, cut into 1-inch strips

1 1/2 teaspoons Lawry's seasoned salt

1 teaspoon garlic powder

1/2 teaspoon freshly ground black pepper

8 tablespoons (1 stick) unsalted butter, melted

1 (6-ounce) bottle Louisiana hot sauce (such as Crystal or Frank's)

For the blue cheese dressing:

1/2 pound crumbled blue cheese (such as Maytag)

1/2 cup light sour cream

1/4 cup Miracle Whip light

Freshly squeezed juice of 1 lemon

1 teaspoon Worcestershire sauce

1 teaspoon honey

1/4 teaspoon cayenne pepper

1/4 teaspoon kosher salt

Celery and carrot sticks

✳ Crispy Dilled Potato Cakes

4 medium Idaho potatoes, cooked and peeled

2 large eggs, lightly beaten

1/4 cup finely chopped fresh dill

2 tablespoons panko bread crumbs (see note, page 19)

1 tablespoon finely chopped scallions

1 teaspoon roasted garlic paste (see box, page 10)

1 teaspoon kosher salt

1/2 teaspoon freshly ground black pepper

Canola oil, as needed

1 cup crème fraîche or sour cream

2 to 4 ounces caviar (depending on your budget)

Potato cakes, flavored with dill and roasted garlic and topped with crème fraîche or sour cream and caviar, make an incredibly decadent appetizer or brunch. You can use salmon, paddlefish, or tobiko roe, which is the tiny beaded flying-fish roe you usually see in sushi restaurants. Or skip the caviar altogether and serve these with sour cream and applesauce, latke-style. That's how they were served when I first fell in love with them, in a Jewish deli in Baltimore.

Makes 6 to 8 servings

1. Using the medium-size holes on a grater, grate the potatoes and set aside in a colander to drain for 5 minutes.

2. In a large bowl, whisk together the eggs, dill, bread crumbs, scallions, garlic paste, salt, and pepper. Gently stir in the potatoes.

3. Using a 1/4-cup measure, form the potato mixture into cakes about 1/4 inch thick. Place on a baking sheet lined with parchment paper.

4. Preheat the oven to 200° F. In a large skillet over medium heat, heat a 1/8-inch layer of oil. Working in batches, making sure not to overcrowd the pan, cook the potato cakes, turning once, until golden brown, about 4 minutes per side. Transfer the cakes to a paper-towel-lined baking sheet and place in the oven. Repeat with the remaining cakes, adding more oil if necessary, making sure the oil is hot before adding the cakes.

5. To serve, place a small dollop of crème fraîche over each cake and top with 1/2 teaspoon of caviar.

Note: Panko Bread Crumbs Typically used in Japanese cooking for coating baked or fried seafood and vegetables, panko crumbs are coarser than most bread crumbs, and result in a much lighter, crispier texture. For this reason, they are swiftly gaining popularity in the United States, and are often readily available in the ethnic section of supermarkets. They can also be purchased online at www.asiangrocer.com.

Crunchy Crab Cakes

After living in Maryland for a few years, I learned to love their version of crab cakes—which I now know is the only way to eat them. They take advantage of the prime blue crabmeat that is readily available and don't use a lot of ingredients that interfere with the meat. My recipe stays true to that version.

Makes 4 servings

1. In a large bowl, whisk together the egg, Worcestershire sauce, lemon juice, parsley, mustard, Old Bay seasoning, and cayenne.

2. Gently fold in the crabmeat and cracker meal, making sure not to break up the crabmeat. Shape the mixture into cakes and refrigerate for at least 30 minutes.

3. Preheat the broiler and transfer the cakes to a broiler-safe pan, keeping them at least 2 inches apart (you may need to cook them in batches). Broil the cakes for 3 minutes, then gently flip them over and broil about 3 minutes more, until they're golden brown. Serve them hot.

Note: Crabmeat You can buy lump crabmeat from a fishmonger, or sometimes you can find it in the freezer section of your supermarket. Let it defrost in the refrigerator overnight if necessary, then use it the same day. You can also buy it online from www.pikeplacefish.com.

1 large egg

1 tablespoon Worcestershire sauce

1 tablespoon freshly squeezed lemon juice

1 tablespoon finely chopped fresh flat-leaf parsley

1 teaspoon Dijon mustard

1 1/2 teaspoons Old Bay seasoning

1/4 teaspoon cayenne pepper

1 pound jumbo lump or lump crabmeat, picked over (see note)

1/4 cup cracker meal

✳ Sumptuous Shrimp with Rosemary and Prosciutto

12 rosemary stalks (cut in half) or wooden skewers

24 U12- or U15-count shrimp, tails on, peeled and deveined (see note)

3 tablespoons extra virgin olive oil

3 tablespoons fresh rosemary leaves, chopped

3 tablespoons fresh thyme leaves

Kosher salt and freshly ground black pepper

8 thin slices imported prosciutto (such as Prosciutto di Parma), cut into thirds

I love serving this dish in the height of summer at barbecues. It's a great alternative to the usual burgers on the grill. It's a good dish for entertaining because you assemble the skewers the day before, then just cook them before serving. The shrimp stays incredibly moist and the prosciutto gets crispy and smoky. If you are having a party, try serving these skewers with a Peachtini. Both the flavors and the colors go really well together. **Makes 6 servings**

1. Soak the rosemary stalks or skewers in water for at least 30 minutes. In a large bowl, combine the shrimp, oil, rosemary, thyme, salt, and pepper, and toss to coat. Marinate in the refrigerator for 15 minutes.

2. Wrap each shrimp snugly in 1 slice of prosciutto. Thread each wrapped shrimp onto a rosemary stalk from head to tail. Refrigerate if not cooking immediately.

3. Preheat the broiler or grill. If broiling, place the shrimp on a baking sheet lined with aluminum foil. Broil them for 1 to 2 minutes per side and serve warm. Alternatively, grill the shrimp until just cooked through, about 1 minute per side.

Note: Shrimp U12- to U15-count shrimp are usually the largest shrimp you can buy. The numbers refer to how many shrimp make up a pound. If you can find only small ones, that's okay, just reduce the cooking time by a minute or two. The thin, black "vein" of a shrimp is actually a digestive tube, and is best removed during preparation. To devein a shrimp, first peel off the shrimp's hard outer shell. Then, using a paring knife, cut a slit along the curved, convex back of the shrimp, from head to tail. Using the tip of your knife, remove the vein under cold running water. Or ask your fishmonger to do it.

Peachtini

Makes 2 servings

1. Fill a shaker halfway with ice. Add the juice, vodka, and schnapps. Cover and shake well for 1 minute.

2. Strain into chilled martini glasses. Garnish each with a peach slice.

5 ounces white peach grape juice

4 ounces premium vodka

3 ounces peach Pucker schnapps

1 white peach, sliced

Spinach Salmon Spring Rolls

For the chili-garlic dipping sauce:

1/2 cup low-sodium soy sauce

3 tablespoons honey

2 tablespoons rice wine vinegar

2 tablespoons freshly squeezed lime juice

2 tablespoons finely chopped fresh cilantro

2 teaspoons toasted (Asian) sesame oil

2 teaspoons Thai chili paste (see note)

1 teaspoon freshly grated ginger

1 teaspoon minced garlic

1 pound salmon fillet, skinned and boned

Kosher salt

1/2 pound fresh baby spinach (about 8 cups)

All-purpose flour, for dusting

20 (8-inch-square) dried rice-paper wrappers (see note)

Peanut oil, for frying

Most spring rolls are filled with a spicy pork-and-vegetable mixture, but since I love fish, I decided to come up with a recipe that uses salmon instead of meat. It's a terrific combination of flavors and textures—spicy and nutty from the chili paste and sesame oil in the dipping sauce, tender inside the rolls from the soft pieces of salmon, and very crunchy from deep-frying. **Makes 10 servings**

1. To make the chili-garlic dipping sauce, in a small bowl, whisk together the soy sauce, honey, vinegar, lime juice, cilantro, sesame oil, chili paste, ginger, and garlic, and mix well.

2. Cut the salmon into thin strips, season with salt, and set aside. Line a large baking sheet with parchment paper and dust with flour.

3. To assemble the spring rolls, gently dip a rice-paper wrapper into a large bowl of warm water until pliable, 10 to 20 seconds. Lay down the rice paper with one corner facing you. Place a couple of spinach leaves toward the bottom of the wrapper. Place 1 strip of salmon on top of the spinach. Bring the corner over the filling, fold in both sides, and continue rolling until it's closed.

4. Place the rolls on the parchment-lined baking sheet, making sure not to let them touch. Repeat until all the ingredients are used. (If you're not frying them immediately, cover the rolls with a dishcloth and refrigerate them for up to 1 hour.)

5. Add about 3 inches of peanut oil to a wok or large pot. Heat the oil to 365° F, or until flour sizzles when sprinkled in. Fry the rolls in batches, about 4 to 6 rolls at a time, depending on the size of the pot. Cook until golden and crisp, 3 to 5 minutes. Transfer them to a paper-towel-lined baking sheet to drain, then serve them hot, with the dipping sauce on the side.

Note: Thai, or Red, Chili Paste Also known as sambal oelek, this simple Asian condiment is a mixture of crushed fresh hot chile peppers and salt. To make your own, remove the seeds from Thai peppers, and finely chop. Grind the mixture in a mortar and pestle with a pinch of salt, and use according to the recipe. Chili paste can also be purchased in Asian grocery stores or online at www.asian grocer.com.

Note: Rice Paper A thin, waferlike wrapper made from a paste of rice and water, rice paper is commonly used in Southeast Asia for the preparation of fresh and fried spring rolls. Usually round or square in shape, it is easily identifiable by the basket-weave texture it acquires from drying on bamboo mats. Rice paper can be found in Asian markets or the ethnic section of the supermarket, or order it online from www.asiangrocer.com.

Super Bowl Salads

Fresh Fruit Salad

Caesar Salad with Rustic Croutons

Romaine Salad with Gorgonzola and Pears

Tomato, Mozzarella, and Basil Salad

Warm Spinach Salad with Bacon Dressing

Roasted Potato and Rosemary Salad

Pasta Salad with Goat Cheese

Everyday Curried Chicken Salad

Southwest Chicken Salad with Chipotle Dressing

Asian Steak Salad with Spicy Vinaigrette

# Fresh Fruit Salad

1 large pineapple, peeled,
cored, and cut into small
chunks

3 large mangoes, peeled,
pitted, and diced

3 Asian pears, peeled, cored,
and diced

6 kiwis, peeled, cut into
1/2-inch rounds, and
quartered

2 cups red seedless grapes,
cut into quarters

2 cups fresh strawberries,
hulled and cut in half

1/4 cup sugar

2 tablespoons vanilla extract

For this salad, I've used some of my favorite fruits, but feel free to use anything ripe and juicy you have on hand. You'll need about fourteen cups of fruit. The vanilla extract is unexpected but gives the fruit a wonderful depth of flavor and some sweetness. This is great for a ladies' brunch and so are the Bellinis, if you want to serve something instead of the usual mimosas to drink. **Makes 10 to 12 servings**

1. In a large bowl, combine the fruit. Add the sugar and vanilla, stirring until the sugar is dissolved.

2. Refrigerate the mixture for 1 hour before serving. Taste and adjust the sugar, if necessary.

Bellini

Makes 4 servings

1 1/2 cups frozen peach slices
(save the nicest 4 for
garnish)

1/4 cup peach schnapps

1 tablespoon grenadine

2 cups Champagne or
sparkling wine

1. In a blender, combine the peaches (except those saved for garnish), schnapps, and grenadine, and blend until well combined.

2. Divide the mixture among 4 Champagne flutes and top each with the Champagne. Stir gently to combine if you like, or you can serve it as is. Garnish each glass with a peach slice, and serve immediately.

Caesar Salad
with Rustic Croutons

A great Caesar salad recipe is hard to find, but this one is a winner. I like to keep it simple and classic and use good ingredients, like the imported Parmigiano-Reggiano cheese, extra virgin olive oil, and nice, tender romaine lettuce. You really can't miss. **Makes 6 servings**

1. Preheat the oven to 350° F. Lay the bread slices flat on a baking sheet and brush the tops with oil. Season the slices with salt and pepper and bake in the top third of the oven about 12 minutes, until crisp and golden.

2. For the dressing, in a blender or a small food processor, combine the oil, 3 tablespoons of the cheese, lemon juice, anchovies, garlic, Worcestershire sauce, honey (if using), and hot sauce. Blend until smooth, and season with salt and pepper to taste.

3. In a large salad bowl, toss the lettuce with the dressing to coat. Sprinkle with the remaining cheese and lots of black pepper. Divide the salad among salad bowls and serve it garnished with the croutons.

For the croutons:

18 (1/2-inch-thick) slices Italian bread (about two-thirds of a large loaf)

1 to 2 tablespoons extra virgin olive oil, for brushing

Kosher salt and freshly ground black pepper

For the dressing:

6 tablespoons extra virgin olive oil

6 tablespoons grated Parmigiano-Reggiano cheese

1/3 cup freshly squeezed lemon juice

3 anchovy fillets

2 garlic cloves

1 tablespoon Worcestershire sauce

2 teaspoons honey, optional

1/2 teaspoon hot sauce, or to taste

Kosher salt and freshly ground black pepper

6 hearts romaine lettuce, ends trimmed, separated into leaves

Romaine Salad with Gorgonzola and Pears

For the candied walnuts:

1/2 cup walnuts

2 teaspoons light corn syrup

1 tablespoon demerara (raw) sugar

For the yogurt dressing:

1/4 cup nonfat yogurt

2 tablespoons buttermilk

2 tablespoons freshly squeezed lemon juice

1 teaspoon roasted garlic paste (see box, page 10), optional

1 teaspoon minced shallot

1 teaspoon honey

1/2 teaspoon kosher salt

1/4 teaspoon freshly ground black pepper

6 cups torn romaine lettuce (about 2 small heads, tough outer leaves discarded)

2 ripe but firm Bartlett pears, peeled, cored, and cubed

1 cup crumbled Gorgonzola or other blue cheese

The idea for this salad came out of my husband's love of blue cheese. Gorgonzola is one of his favorites, but you can use any blue cheese you like. You can make this with or without candied walnuts. It tastes great both ways, but Tony loves the nuts, since they add that all-important crunch. You can make them ahead and they last for weeks—if you don't eat them all, that is. **Makes 4 servings**

1. To prepare the candied walnuts, preheat the oven to 325° F. Spread the nuts out on a baking pan and toast, stirring once or twice, about 10 minutes, until light golden brown. Transfer the nuts to a bowl, and let cool.

2. Toss the nuts with the corn syrup and then with the sugar. Spread them out again on the baking sheet and bake about 10 minutes, until golden and fragrant. Cool completely before serving.

3. For the dressing, combine the yogurt, buttermilk, lemon juice, garlic paste, shallot, honey, salt, and pepper in a blender, and blend until smooth. Taste and adjust the seasoning if necessary. The dressing can be refrigerated in a covered container for up to 4 days.

4. In a salad bowl, toss the greens with about 3 tablespoons of the dressing, enough to lightly coat the salad. Add the pears and cheese and toss again, adding more dressing to taste. Garnish with candied walnuts.

✳ Tomato, Mozzarella, and Basil Salad

Tony's new favorite salad is Caprese, the classic Italian combination of fresh, milky mozzarella with tomatoes and basil. It's a simple salad that's all about the quality of the ingredients. When heirloom tomatoes are in season I use a variety of those, since nothing beats their sweet juiciness, and I always bring out my best olive oil for this. It's also worth seeking out aged balsamic vinegar. The older it is, the thicker and sweeter it gets. If you get one that's really old and syrupy, you don't have to reduce it. Just drizzle on enough to coat the tomatoes. **Makes 4 to 6 servings**

1 cup aged balsamic vinegar

2 pounds halved cherry tomatoes or cubed heirloom tomatoes (a mixture of red, yellow, and orange)

1 pound buffalo milk bocconcini, halved (see note)

1/2 bunch (about 1/2 cup) fresh basil leaves, torn

Kosher salt and freshly ground black pepper

2 tablespoons extra virgin olive oil

1. In a small saucepan over low heat, cook the balsamic vinegar until it is reduced by half and coats the back of a spoon, 15 to 20 minutes. Remove from the heat and let cool.

2. In a large bowl, combine the tomatoes, mozzarella, and basil, and salt and freshly ground pepper to taste. Place the salad in the center of a plate and drizzle with just enough balsamic syrup and olive oil to coat. Top with more ground pepper, if desired, and serve immediately. Leftover salad can be stored in an airtight container in the refrigerator for up to 2 days.

Note: Bocconcini Bocconcini, Italian for "little mouthfuls," are bite-size balls of mozzarella. Use buffalo milk mozzarella if you can find it; it has a richer flavor. But regular cow's milk mozzarella is fine, too. The most important thing is that the bocconcini are fresh, because the fresher they are, the milkier—and more delicious—they will taste. If bocconcini are not available, feel free to cube up a pound of regular fresh mozzarella.

Warm Spinach Salad
with Bacon Dressing

For the warm bacon vinaigrette:

5 slices bacon

1 tablespoon minced shallot

1 teaspoon minced garlic

1/2 cup red wine vinegar

1 tablespoon Dijon mustard

1 to 2 teaspoons honey, to taste

Kosher salt and freshly ground black pepper

1/2 pound fresh baby spinach (about 8 cups)

6 ounces thinly sliced button mushrooms (about 2 cups)

1/2 cup thinly sliced red onion

You can never go wrong with this classic salad. The combination of smoky bacon, tender spinach, crisp onions, and a sweet-tart dressing is about as good as salad gets.

Makes 4 servings

1. To make the vinaigrette, in a large skillet over medium heat, cook the bacon until crisp, 5 to 7 minutes. Transfer the bacon to a paper-towel-lined plate to drain. Discard all but 2 tablespoons of the fat. Crumble the bacon when it's cool enough to handle.

2. In the remaining fat, sauté the shallot for 1 minute. Add the garlic and sauté for 30 seconds. Whisk in the vinegar, mustard, honey, and salt and pepper to taste. Bring the liquid to a boil, then remove from the heat. Taste the dressing and adjust the seasoning if necessary.

3. To make the salad, in a large bowl, combine the spinach, mushrooms, onion, and salt and pepper to taste. Toss the greens with enough vinaigrette to lightly coat the salad. Garnish with the crumbled bacon and serve immediately, adding more dressing to taste.

Roasted Potato and Rosemary Salad

'm not a huge fan of the classic potato salad with mayo, so I came up with this sensational recipe and everyone loves it. The roasted potatoes make this really unique, and the mustard-and-rosemary dressing adds plenty of flavor. And, unlike regular potato salad, it's perfect for picnics and barbecues on hot days, when leaving anything with mayo outside can be problematic. **Makes 6 servings**

1. Preheat the oven to 375° F. In a large roasting pan, toss together the potatoes, 1 tablespoon of the olive oil, and salt and pepper to taste. Roast until the potatoes are fork-tender, 30 to 45 minutes, depending on the size. Transfer to a large bowl.

2. In a small bowl, whisk together the lime juice, mustard, remaining olive oil, garlic paste, scallions, rosemary, and honey. Taste and adjust the seasoning if necessary. Pour the dressing over the warm potatoes and serve warm or at room temperature.

2 pounds new red potatoes, cut in half

3 tablespoons extra virgin olive oil

Kosher salt and freshly ground black pepper

Freshly squeezed juice of 1 lime

2 tablespoons Dijon mustard

2 teaspoons roasted garlic paste (see box, page 10)

4 scallions, chopped

Leaves from 4 sprigs fresh rosemary, finely chopped

1 teaspoon honey, or to taste

Pasta Salad with Goat Cheese

6 ounces arugula

4 ounces crumbled goat or
feta cheese

1/3 cup Kalamata olives, pitted
and sliced

1/3 cup green olives, pitted
and sliced

3 tablespoons oil-packed
sun-dried tomatoes,
drained and sliced

1 tablespoon capers, rinsed
and drained

1 pound fusilli pasta

2 tablespoons extra virgin
olive oil

1 tablespoon red wine vinegar

2 teaspoons roasted garlic
paste (see box, page 10)

Freshly squeezed juice of
1 lemon

1/4 teaspoon crushed red
pepper flakes

Kosher salt and freshly
ground black pepper

6 fresh basil leaves, cut into
a chiffonade (see note)

My mom used to make a great but pretty simple pasta salad when I was growing up. This is a gourmet version of that, packed with goat cheese, arugula, olives, sun-dried tomatoes, capers, and basil. Everyone loves it. It has great flavor and very little fat. **Makes 8 servings**

1. Bring a large pot of salted water to a boil. In a large bowl, combine the arugula, cheese, olives, tomatoes, and capers. Cover tightly with plastic wrap and refrigerate until needed, up to 1 hour.

2. Cook the pasta until al dente, 6 to 8 minutes, and drain well. Meanwhile, in a small bowl, whisk together the olive oil, vinegar, garlic paste, lemon juice, and crushed red pepper. Taste and adjust the seasoning if necessary.

3. Season the arugula mixture with salt and pepper to taste. Add the pasta to the salad and toss with the dressing. Taste and adjust the seasoning if necessary. Add the basil just before serving, and serve warm or at room temperature.

Note: Chiffonade Making a chiffonade is easy, and the delicate ribbons of herbs look much nicer than simply rough-chopping them. Remove the leaves from the stem, stack up the leaves evenly, and roll the stack into a tight bunch. Using a sharp knife, slice the roll crosswise into fine strips.

Everyday Curried Chicken Salad

Toasting the curry powder takes this salad to a whole other level, flavor-wise, and using store-bought roasted chicken will save tons of time. I love the sweet burst of the grapes, but you can omit them if you wish. Make sure to buy fresh curry powder if yours has been sitting in the cabinet for more than a year. It makes a big difference. Serve the salad as a filling for pitas or croissants, or over a bed of greens. **Makes 8 servings**

1. Heat a small pan over medium heat for 1 minute. Add the curry powder and stir until it starts to release its scent, about 30 seconds. Transfer to a small bowl and let cool.

2. In a large bowl, combine the chicken, grapes, celery, onion, parsley, and salt and pepper to taste, and toss gently.

3. Add the Miracle Whip, mustard, lemon juice, garlic paste, and honey to the bowl with the curry powder and whisk until smooth. Taste and adjust the seasoning if necessary. Pour the curry dressing over the chicken and toss gently to coat.

1 1/2 tablespoons Madras curry powder

2 whole roasted chickens, skinned, boned, and torn into bite-size pieces (about 8 cups)

2 cups green grapes, cut in half, optional

1 cup chopped celery

1/2 cup minced red onion

1/2 cup chopped fresh flat-leaf parsley

Kosher salt and freshly ground black pepper

3/4 cup Miracle Whip light or low-fat mayonnaise

2 tablespoons Dijon mustard

Freshly squeezed juice of 1 lemon

2 teaspoons roasted garlic paste (see box, page 10)

2 teaspoons honey, or to taste

Southwest Chicken Salad
with Chipotle Dressing

2 ears fresh corn

Cooking spray or melted butter

4 skinless, boneless chicken thighs

1 tablespoon ancho chile powder (see note)

1 tablespoon ground cumin

1 1/2 teaspoons ground coriander

1 1/2 teaspoons garlic powder

Kosher salt and freshly ground black pepper

6 cups mixed baby greens

2 medium roasted, peeled, and seeded red bell peppers (see box, page 51), julienned

1 cup canned black beans, rinsed and drained

1 cup julienned jicama

1/2 cup chopped fresh cilantro

When it comes to food, Tony's a texture guy. He likes things with crunch or, ideally, a mix of crunchy, creamy, and juicy. This salad has it all—great crunch from the jicama, creaminess from the beans, and juiciness from the corn—and it's also hearty, filling, colorful, and healthy. No wonder it's one of his favorite salads. **Makes 4 servings**

1. To roast the corn, preheat the oven to 400° F. Soak the corn in water, husks on, for 30 minutes. Peel back the husks, remove the silk, and re-cover corn with the husks. Place the corn directly on the oven rack. Cook for 30 minutes, turning halfway through the cooking time. Remove from the oven, let cool, then peel back the husks and cut the corn kernels from the cob.

2. Place a cooking rack in the upper third of the oven. Preheat the broiler to high. Cover a baking sheet with foil and spray the sheet with cooking spray or brush with melted butter. Arrange the chicken on the baking sheet.

3. In a small bowl, combine the chile powder, cumin, coriander, and garlic powder, and mix well. Season the chicken on both sides with salt and pepper, and sprinkle the spice mixture liberally on both sides. Spray the chicken with cooking spray or brush with melted butter. Place under the broiler, and cook for 5 minutes on each side or until cooked through. Transfer to a plate to cool.

4. In a large bowl, combine the corn kernels, greens, red peppers, black beans, jicama, and cilantro. Season the salad with salt and pepper to taste, and toss well.

5. To make the dressing, in a blender, combine the Miracle Whip, yogurt, lime juice, garlic paste, mustard, honey (if using), chipotle pepper, and salt, and blend until smooth. Taste and adjust the seasoning if necessary.

6. Toss the salad with about 3 tablespoons of dressing, enough to lightly coat the salad. Thinly slice the chicken. Place a mound of salad on each plate and top with the chicken. Drizzle extra dressing over the salad, if desired.

Note: Ancho Chile Powder The dried version of the triangular-shaped Mexican poblano pepper, ancho chiles are used extensively in Mexican cooking. Blackish-purple in color, with a mild, sweet heat, ancho chiles are available whole and powdered at Hispanic grocery stores or online at www.penzeys.com.

Note: Chipotle Chile A staple in Mexican cooking, chipotle chiles are simply jalapeños that have been smoked. Available dried, powdered, pickled, or canned in adobo sauce (a blend of tomatoes, vinegar, and spices), chipotles are found in the ethnic section of most supermarkets. If you like your chiles hot, use canned chipotles straight out of the sauce. If you prefer a milder flavor, the chile can be rinsed, seeded, and patted dry before chopping.

For the chipotle dressing:

1/4 cup Miracle Whip light or mayonnaise

1/4 cup nonfat yogurt, drained

Freshly squeezed juice of 2 limes, plus additional to taste

1 tablespoon roasted garlic paste (see box, page 10)

1 tablespoon Dijon mustard

1 tablespoon honey, or to taste, optional

1 canned chipotle chile in adobo sauce (see note)

1/2 teaspoon kosher salt

Asian Steak Salad
with Spicy Vinaigrette

1/4 cup low-sodium soy sauce

Freshly squeezed juice and finely grated zest of 1 lime

2 tablespoons minced ginger

1 tablespoon roasted garlic paste (see box, page 10)

2 teaspoons toasted (Asian) sesame oil

1 pound flank steak

2 carrots, julienned

1/2 red bell pepper, julienned

1/2 English cucumber, sliced

1/4 head romaine lettuce, cored and thinly sliced (about 2 1/2 cups)

1/4 head red cabbage, cored and thinly sliced (about 2 1/2 cups)

1/4 cup chopped fresh cilantro

Kosher salt and freshly ground black pepper

2 tablespoons chopped peanuts, optional

For the spicy vinaigrette:

2 tablespoons low-sodium soy sauce

2 tablespoons rice wine vinegar

2 tablespoons canola oil

1 tablespoon Thai or Vietnamese fish sauce (see note)

Freshly squeezed juice of 1 lime

1 teaspoon red chili paste (see note, page 23)

1 teaspoon honey

1 garlic clove, minced

When it comes to feeding my man, putting meat in just about anything makes him happy. But this crunchy salad works for me, too, because it's filled with lots of veggies. It's great to serve with Mai Tais since their sweetness plays really well off the tanginess of the dressing. Bonus: You can prep all the veggies the day before and keep them in plastic bags in the refrigerator until you're ready to serve.

Makes 4 servings

1. To make the marinade, whisk together the soy sauce, lime juice and zest, ginger, garlic paste, and sesame oil. Place the steak in a shallow dish and cover with the marinade, turning completely to coat. Cover the dish with plastic wrap and refrigerate for at least 1 hour and up to 12 hours. Remove the steak from the refrigerator 30 minutes prior to cooking.

2. In a large bowl, combine the carrots, bell pepper, cucumber, lettuce, cabbage, cilantro, and peanuts, and toss well. Cover tightly with plastic wrap and refrigerate for up to 3 hours.

3. To make the vinaigrette, in a small bowl, whisk together the soy sauce, vinegar, oil, fish sauce, lime juice, chili paste, honey, and garlic.

4. Heat a grill or grill pan over medium-high heat. Remove the steak from the marinade, and season with salt and pepper. Sear the steak until browned, turning once, 4 to 5 minutes per side for medium-rare. Transfer the steak to a cutting board and let it rest for 5 minutes. Thinly slice the steak against the grain.

5. To assemble, add 3 tablespoons of vinaigrette to the salad and toss well. Add more dressing, if desired. Place the salad on the center of a dinner plate and top with several slices of steak. Sprinkle with the chopped peanuts, if desired, drizzle with more vinaigrette, and serve.

Note: Thai or Vietnamese Fish Sauce Thai or Vietnamese fish sauce (called "nam pla" in Thai and "nuoc mam" in Vietnamese) is a primary ingredient in Southeast Asian cooking. Prepared from fermented anchovies, its strong, salty flavor and pungent aroma can intimidate those unaccustomed to cooking with it, but when combined with other Asian ingredients, fish sauce lends a subtle, complex flavor that enriches many soups, noodles, and sauces. You can use either Thai or Vietnamese brands interchangeably. Fish sauce can be found in Asian markets or purchased online at www.templeofthai.com.

Mai Tai

Makes 4 servings

1. Fill a large cocktail shaker halfway with ice. Add the light rum, pineapple juice, brandy, Grand Marnier, orange juice, lime juice, and grenadine. Cover and shake well for 30 seconds.

2. Fill 4 cocktail glasses with ice. Strain the mai tai into each glass. Top with 1/2 ounce of dark rum per glass. Garnish each glass with a pineapple wedge and a cherry.

8 ounces light rum

6 ounces pineapple juice

2 ounces apricot brandy

2 ounces Grand Marnier or triple sec

2 ounces orange juice

Freshly squeezed juice of 1 lime

1 ounce grenadine

2 ounces dark rum

4 pineapple wedges

4 maraschino cherries

Warm-ups: Soups and Stews

Split Pea Soup with Crispy Prosciutto

2 tablespoons extra virgin olive oil

2 ounces sliced prosciutto, cut crosswise into 1/4-inch strips

2 carrots, chopped

1 small onion, chopped

1 celery stalk, chopped

2 garlic cloves, chopped

6 cups low-sodium chicken broth or stock, plus additional to thin the soup, as needed

2 cups (about 1 pound) green split peas, picked over and rinsed

1 bay leaf

Kosher salt and freshly ground black pepper

My mom made split pea soup when I was growing up, and it was always just perfect for those cold winter days. My recipe is pretty much the same as hers, except I substitute prosciutto for the usual ham, fry it until it's crunchy, and use it as a garnish. It's a thick, savory, and very tasty bowl of soup.

A note about cooking the peas—the cooking time will vary depending on how old they are, and how they have been stored. The soup is done when the peas are completely tender and have absorbed most of the liquid. This can take anywhere from forty-five minutes to an hour and a half, so taste for doneness rather than judging by time alone. If the soup is getting too dry and the peas aren't done, stir in a little more broth or water and continue cooking. **Makes 6 servings**

1. In a large Dutch oven over medium heat, warm the oil. Separate the prosciutto strips, then fry them in the oil, tossing frequently, until crisp, 5 to 6 minutes. Use a slotted spoon to transfer the prosciutto to a paper-towel-lined plate. Add the carrots, onion, and celery to the pot, and cook, stirring, until softened, about 6 minutes. Add the garlic and cook, stirring, for 30 seconds more.

2. Add the chicken broth, split peas, and bay leaf, and bring the soup to a boil. Reduce the heat to low and simmer gently, partially covered, until the peas are completely tender, about 1 hour. Season with salt and pepper to taste. Discard the bay leaf.

3. Serve bowls of the soup garnished with the crispy prosciutto strips.

✳ French Onion Soup

French onion soup has always been one of Tony's favorites, and he used to order it at every restaurant he could, whenever he saw it on the menu. Then, one night several years ago, I surprised him with a big pot of it when he came home from work. Since then I've made it often—especially during Tony's rookie year in the league, when he craved it all the time. It takes a lot of patience to caramelize onions, but it's worth it. The soup itself can be made a day in advance; just don't garnish it with the herbs or cheese croutons until you are ready to serve it. **Makes 8 servings**

2 tablespoons unsalted butter

8 large sweet onions (preferably a mix of Vidalia and red), thickly sliced

1/4 cup Cognac or brandy

2 tablespoons dry vermouth

8 cups low-sodium beef broth or stock

4 sprigs fresh thyme

2 bay leaves

Kosher salt and freshly ground black pepper

1/4 cup finely chopped fresh flat-leaf parsley

1/4 cup chopped scallions

8 (1/2-inch-thick) baguette slices

8 slices Gruyère cheese (4 to 6 ounces)

1. In a wide stockpot or large Dutch oven, melt the butter over medium-low heat. Add the onions and cook, stirring occasionally, until they are very soft and have turned golden (raise the heat if the onions exude a lot of liquid), 45 minutes to 1 hour.

2. Pour the Cognac and vermouth into the pan, and cook, stirring, until the liquid has reduced to a glaze, 1 to 3 minutes. Add the beef broth, thyme, bay leaves, and salt and pepper to taste. Bring the soup to a boil, then reduce the heat and simmer gently, uncovered, for 30 minutes. Taste and adjust the seasoning if necessary. Discard the thyme sprigs and bay leaves. Stir in the parsley and scallions.

3. Put a rack in the top third of the oven and preheat the broiler. Arrange the baguette slices on a baking sheet and broil until toasted. Take the pan out of the oven but leave the broiler on.

4. Ladle the soup into ovenproof crocks, leaving an inch of space at the top. Set a slice of baguette, toasted side down, on the surface of each bowl of soup. Place the crocks on a baking sheet, top the baguette slices with cheese, and broil until the cheese is bubbling and golden, 1 to 2 minutes. Serve immediately.

Gran's Get-Well Chicken Soup

(From my grandmother Jacqueline Warr)

For the chicken stock:

1 (3- to 4-pound) chicken, with neck (giblets removed)

2 celery stalks, cut into chunks

1 head garlic, skin on, halved crosswise

1 small onion, halved

1 carrot, cut into chunks

1 parsnip, cut into chunks

10 sprigs fresh flat-leaf parsley

10 whole black peppercorns

2 teaspoons kosher salt

2 bay leaves, crushed

For the soup:

2 tablespoons canola oil

1 cup chopped onions

1 cup chopped celery

1 cup chopped carrots

Kosher salt and freshly ground black pepper

8 ounces broad egg noodles

1/4 cup chopped fresh flat-leaf parsley

My gran always knew how to heal a cold—with a big bowl of old-fashioned chicken noodle soup. Add a side of saltine crackers and you're on your way to recovery. You don't have to be sick, however, to make or eat this. It's perfect anytime you want something homey and warming.

Makes 8 servings

1. For the stock, place the chicken in a stockpot with cold water to cover (about 12 cups). Add the remaining ingredients and bring to a boil. Reduce the heat to medium-low and cook, uncovered, at a slow simmer until the chicken begins to fall apart, 1 to 1¼ hours. Transfer the chicken to a plate to cool.

2. Strain the stock into a large bowl, discarding the solids. (The stock can be cooled and refrigerated for up to 3 days at this point; remove the fat once it has hardened.) Skim most of the fat from the surface of the liquid.

3. When the chicken is cool enough to handle, remove its skin and pull the meat into bite-size pieces.

4. Wipe out the stockpot, place it over medium heat, and add the oil. Add the onions, celery, and carrots, and cook, stirring, until the vegetables begin to soften, 6 to 8 minutes. Add the skimmed stock and additional salt and pepper to taste, and bring to a boil.

5. Stir the noodles and reserved chicken meat into the soup, and boil until the noodles are barely done, about 6 minutes. Add the parsley and serve. Leftovers freeze well for about 1 month.

✳ Roasted Tomato Bisque with Brie Toasts

As a kid, I loved having tomato soup and grilled cheese for lunch. This is the adult version of that favorite meal. Made with plenty of tomatoes but only a little cream, it's light for a bisque recipe, but still filling and flavorful. This is because I char the tomatoes under the broiler before adding them to the soup, which gives them a slightly smoky taste. If fresh tomatoes aren't in season, use two large (28-ounce) cans of whole plum tomatoes instead. **Makes 6 servings**

1. Preheat the broiler and spread the tomatoes, cut side down, on a baking sheet lined with foil. Place the tomatoes directly under the broiler and cook until charred, 10 to 12 minutes, then set aside.

2. Meanwhile, heat a medium stockpot over medium heat, and add the oil. Stir in the onion and cook, stirring frequently, until golden brown, about 7 minutes. Add the garlic, thyme, bay leaves, and crushed red pepper, and cook for 30 seconds.

3. Add the chicken broth, sherry, tomatoes, honey, salt, and pepper. Bring to a boil, then reduce the heat to medium-low. Cook, uncovered, until the soup has thickened, about 40 minutes.

4. Taste and adjust the seasoning if necessary. Remove the thyme sprigs and bay leaves and discard them. Puree the soup using a blender or an immersion blender. Return the soup to the pot, if necessary, and place over medium heat. Add the cream and simmer for 5 minutes.

5. Place the baguette slices on a baking sheet and top with the cheese. Place under the broiler for 30 seconds or until the cheese melts.

6. Ladle the soup into bowls and top with the basil. Serve 2 pieces of Brie toast with each bowl of bisque.

2 pounds plum tomatoes, halved and seeded

2 tablespoons extra virgin olive oil

1 small onion, thinly sliced

2 garlic cloves, minced

3 sprigs fresh thyme

2 bay leaves

1/4 teaspoon crushed red pepper flakes

2 cups low-sodium chicken broth or stock

2 tablespoons dry sherry

1/2 to 1 tablespoon honey, to taste

1 1/2 teaspoons kosher salt

Freshly ground black pepper

1/3 cup heavy cream

8 (1/2-inch-thick) baguette slices, toasted

1/2 pound Brie cheese, cut into 8 (1/4-inch-thick) slices

2 tablespoons fresh basil leaves, cut into a chiffonade (see note, page 32)

Shrimp Bisque

4 tablespoons extra virgin olive oil

2 pounds medium shrimp, cleaned (reserve shells) and deveined (see note, page 20)

1 teaspoon kosher salt, plus additional for seasoning the shrimp

1/4 teaspoon cayenne pepper, plus additional for seasoning the shrimp

1 bay leaf

1 teaspoon dried thyme

1/2 cup dry or sweet sherry, to taste

5 cups fish stock or vegetable broth

1/4 cup all-purpose flour

1 cup chopped sweet onions (such as Vidalia or red)

1/2 cup chopped celery

1/2 cup chopped red bell pepper

2 garlic cloves, minced

1 (12-ounce) can evaporated skim milk

1 tablespoon Worcestershire sauce

Dash of hot sauce

I never actually go on a diet, but I always try to find little ways to eliminate unnecessary fat in the foods I cook. For this bisque recipe, I've substituted evaporated skim milk for the usual cream. Then I kick up the flavor by cooking the shrimp shells in the broth. It lends an incredible seafood taste to the dish. **Makes 6 servings**

1. In a large stockpot, heat 1 tablespoon of the oil over medium heat. Season the shrimp with salt and cayenne to taste. Add the shrimp to the pot and cook until just pink but not cooked through, about 2 minutes. Transfer to a plate and set aside.

2. To the same pan, add the shrimp shells, bay leaf, and thyme, and cook until the shells turn pink, about 2 minutes. Add the sherry and cook until it reduces by half, 2 to 3 minutes. Add the stock and bring to a boil. Cover, reduce the heat to low, and simmer for 20 minutes. Strain the broth into a large bowl, discarding the shells, thyme, and bay leaf.

3. Return the pan to medium heat and add the remaining olive oil. Whisk in the flour. Cook, stirring constantly, until the roux turns golden, 3 to 5 minutes. Add the onions, celery, and bell pepper. Cook until the vegetables are very tender, about 15 minutes. Add the garlic and cook for 30 seconds.

4. Gradually add the reserved broth, whisking until blended. Bring to a boil and reduce the heat to medium-low. Add the milk, the teaspoon of salt, and ¼ teaspoon of cayenne, and simmer until the bisque thickens, about 20 minutes. Taste and adjust the seasoning if necessary.

5. Using an immersion blender or working in batches in a regular blender, blend the bisque until it's almost smooth. Return to the pot if necessary. Add the shrimp, Worcestershire sauce, and hot sauce, and cook until the shrimp is just done, about 3 minutes.

Creamy Crab and Corn Chowder

This velvety soup is my low-fat version of a classic corn chowder, made extra flavorful with a good dose of crabmeat. If the soup gets too thick, which it might, especially if you make it ahead and reheat it, add water until it reaches the desired consistency. **Makes 8 servings**

1. In a Dutch oven over medium-high heat, cook the bacon until crisp, about 5 minutes. With a slotted spoon, transfer the bacon to a paper-towel-lined plate. Add the onion, celery, and carrot to the pot and cook, stirring, until soft, about 10 minutes. Add the garlic and cook 30 seconds more.

2. Stir in the chicken broth, potatoes, and thyme, and bring to a boil. Reduce the heat and simmer for 10 minutes.

3. Add the corn kernels, cream-style corn, evaporated milk (reserving 4 tablespoons), salt, and cayenne. Bring the mixture to a boil, then reduce the heat to medium-low. Cook, uncovered, until the potatoes are fork-tender, about 20 minutes. In a small bowl, whisk together the remaining evaporated milk and the flour. Add this mixture in a slow stream to the pot, stirring constantly.

4. Cook until slightly thickened, about 10 minutes. Gently stir in the crabmeat and cook until heated through, about 5 minutes more. Taste and adjust the seasoning if necessary. Add the reserved bacon and the parsley and serve hot.

4 slices bacon, cut into 1/2-inch pieces

1/2 cup chopped onion

1/4 cup chopped celery

1/4 cup chopped carrot

2 garlic cloves, minced

4 cups low-sodium chicken broth or stock

1 pound red potatoes, cubed

2 teaspoons dried thyme

2 cups fresh or frozen corn kernels

1 (15-ounce) can cream-style corn

1 (12-ounce) can evaporated skim milk, 4 tablespoons reserved

1 teaspoon kosher salt

1/4 teaspoon cayenne pepper

2 tablespoons all-purpose flour

1 pound lump crabmeat, picked clean (see page 19)

1/4 cup chopped fresh flat-leaf parsley

Jambalaya

1 teaspoon extra virgin
   olive oil

1 pound andouille sausage,
   diced large (see note)

4 (4- to 6-ounce) boneless,
   skinless chicken thighs,
   cut into chunks

Kosher salt and freshly
   ground black pepper

1½ cups chopped Spanish
   onions

1 cup chopped green bell
   pepper

1 cup chopped red bell pepper

½ cup chopped celery

2 tablespoons minced garlic

1 tablespoon paprika

½ tablespoon dried oregano

1 teaspoon cayenne pepper

3 bay leaves

4 cups low-sodium chicken
   broth or stock

2 cups peeled, seeded, and
   chopped tomatoes, drained
   (see box)

2 tablespoons Worcestershire
   sauce

2 cups long-grain rice,
   uncooked

2 pounds large shrimp, peeled
   and deveined (see note,
   page 20)

½ cup chopped scallions,
   plus additional for garnish

¼ cup chopped fresh flat-leaf
   parsley, plus additional for
   garnish

Jambalaya is a traditional Louisiana stew originally made from whatever people had around their kitchens, from chicken to shrimp to vegetables, as long as it was spiked with chile, flavored with onion, tomato, and bell pepper, and bulked out with rice. In my version, I use a combination of sausage, shrimp, and chicken, which makes an extremely hearty dish that's perfect for a crowd. **Makes 8 servings**

1. In a Dutch oven or large pot over medium-high heat, warm the oil. Add the sausage and cook, stirring occasionally, until the fat has rendered, about 5 minutes. Remove the sausage from the pan with a slotted spoon, and transfer to a paper-towel-lined plate.

2. Season the chicken with salt and pepper. Add the chicken to the pan and cook, stirring occasionally, until lightly browned, about 3 minutes per side. With a slotted spoon, transfer the chicken to the paper-towel-lined plate with the sausage.

3. To the same pan, add the onions, bell peppers, and celery. Reduce the heat to medium and cook the vegetables until soft, about 7 minutes.

4. Stir in the garlic, paprika, oregano, cayenne, and bay leaves, and cook, stirring, for about 1 minute. Add the broth, tomatoes, and Worcestershire sauce, and bring to a boil. Add the rice and reserved sausage and chicken to the pan. Reduce the heat to low, cover, and simmer until the rice is tender, 15 to 20 minutes.

5. Taste and adjust the seasoning if necessary. Raise the heat to medium. Season the shrimp with salt, add it to the rice mixture, and cook until the shrimp is just cooked through, about 5 minutes. Add the scallions and parsley and stir to combine. Serve family-style in a large bowl, garnished with additional scallions and parsley.

Note: Andouille Andouille is a spicy, garlicky smoked Cajun sausage made of pork. It originated in France and was brought to Louisiana, where it became a mainstay, and it is integral in recipes for gumbo, jambalaya, and red beans and rice. If it is not available, substitute spicy Italian sausage for a different flavor, or order andouille online from www.cajunmarket.com.

How to Peel and Seed Tomatoes

To peel and seed a tomato, bring a pot of water to a boil and fill a large bowl with ice water. Using a paring knife, make a small shallow X on the bottom of the tomato. Drop the tomato in the boiling water for 10 seconds. Remove the tomato with a slotted spoon and transfer it immediately to the bowl of water. Peel off the skin with the paring knife, and slice the tomato in half crosswise. Remove the seeds with a spoon (or gently squeeze the tomato with your hands), and chop the tomato to the desired size. (Alternatively, you can substitute canned diced tomatoes here; just drain them before measuring.)

Everyday Maryland Crab Soup

2 tablespoons extra virgin olive oil

1 1/2 cups chopped onions

1 cup chopped green bell pepper

3 tablespoons minced garlic

2 (28-ounce) cans diced tomatoes

3 cups low-sodium chicken broth or stock

1 (16-ounce) bag frozen carrot, green bean, corn, and pea mix

1 (6-ounce) can tomato paste

2 tablespoons Old Bay seasoning

2 tablespoons Worcestershire sauce

1 tablespoon sugar, or to taste, optional

2 teaspoons dried thyme

1/2 teaspoon cayenne pepper

2 bay leaves

Dash of hot sauce

2 pounds lump crabmeat, picked clean (see note, page 19)

Freshly squeezed juice of 1 lemon

1/4 cup chopped fresh flat-leaf parsley

Every restaurant and deli in and around Maryland has a version of this soup; this one is mine. It's an easy recipe that's great for cooking up after work, though you can also make it ahead. In fact, as with many soups, it tastes better the following day, when the flavors have had a chance to come together. Serve with crusty bread. **Makes 8 servings**

1. In a large stockpot over medium-high heat, warm the oil. Add the onions and bell pepper and cook, stirring occasionally, until soft, about 10 minutes. Add the garlic and cook for 30 seconds.

2. Add the stewed tomatoes, chicken broth, frozen vegetables, tomato paste, Old Bay, Worcestershire sauce, sugar (if using), thyme, cayenne, bay leaves, and hot sauce. Bring to a boil, cover, and reduce the heat to medium-low. Simmer until the vegetables are soft, about 30 minutes. Discard bay leaves.

3. Taste and adjust the seasoning if necessary. Add the crabmeat and lemon juice and stir gently. Cook for 10 minutes more. Add the parsley and serve hot.

Spicy Latin Fish Stew

I was in heaven when I lived in Miami. Not just because of the beach, but because of the plethora of fresh, inexpensive fish. There was always something interesting in the market, and I did a lot of experimenting. That's where I came up with the recipe for this spicy dish, which is pretty light for a stew, but heartier than a soup. I think it's perfect to eat in the summer since it won't weigh you down. If you like it really spicy, don't seed the jalapeños. **Makes 6 to 8 servings**

1. In a food processor, puree the tomatoes, 1 cup of the onions, the cilantro, parsley, lime juice, canola oil, jalapeño, garlic, salt, and several grinds of black pepper until smooth. Place the fish and shrimp in separate nonreactive bowls and pour the puree over them to cover. Cover the bowls tightly with plastic wrap and refrigerate for 1 hour.

2. In a large Dutch oven, combine the remaining cup of onions with the peppers, chicken broth, and bay leaf. Bring to a boil and simmer, covered, until the vegetables begin to soften, about 4 minutes.

3. Uncover the pot, stir in the fish and puree, and simmer gently until the fish is opaque, 4 to 6 minutes. Add the shrimp and puree, and continue to simmer until the shrimp turn pink and the fish is just cooked, about 1 minute more. Discard bay leaf. Taste and season with additional salt and pepper if needed.

4. Serve immediately, garnished with cilantro and parsley and accompanied by lime wedges.

1 (28-ounce) can tomatoes

2 cups chopped white onions

1/4 cup chopped fresh cilantro, plus additional for garnish

1/4 cup chopped fresh flat-leaf parsley, plus additional for garnish

1/4 cup freshly squeezed lime juice, plus lime wedges for serving

3 tablespoons canola oil

1 jalapeño pepper, seeded (unless more heat is desired)

1 large garlic clove

1 1/2 teaspoons kosher salt

Freshly ground black pepper

2 1/2 pounds boneless, skinless, firm white fish fillets (such as cod, haddock, flounder, or scrod)

1 pound medium shrimp, halved lengthwise and deveined (see note, page 20)

1 green bell pepper, chopped

1 red bell pepper, chopped

1 cup low-sodium chicken broth or stock

1 bay leaf

Chicken Chili with Roasted Peppers

3 tablespoons extra virgin olive oil

1 1/2 pounds skinless, boneless chicken, either light or dark meat, diced

Kosher salt and freshly ground black pepper

1 medium red onion, chopped

1 celery stalk, chopped

1 carrot, chopped

1 small roasted, peeled, seeded, and chopped red bell pepper (see box)

1 small roasted, peeled, seeded, and chopped green bell pepper (see box)

4 garlic cloves, roasted, peeled, and chopped (see box)

2 jalapeño peppers, roasted, peeled, seeded, and finely chopped (see box)

1 tablespoon ancho chile powder (see note, page 35)

2 teaspoons ground cumin

1 teaspoon dried oregano

1/4 teaspoon ground cinnamon

2 (15-ounce) cans stewed tomatoes, with juice

2 cups low-sodium chicken broth or stock

1 cup canned pinto beans, rinsed and drained

1 cup canned black beans, rinsed and drained

1 cup fresh or frozen corn kernels

This is similar to my mother's chili recipe (see page 52) except here I use chicken instead of turkey and add roasted bell peppers. It's an unexpected combination that really has complexity. Using white-meat chicken keeps the dish relatively low-fat, but dark meat chicken has more flavor, so you can decide. Naturally, serve this with cornbread. **Makes 8 servings**

1. In a Dutch oven over medium-high heat, warm the olive oil. Season the chicken generously with salt and pepper. Add the chicken to the oil in batches, and brown on both sides, about 8 minutes for each batch. Set aside.

2. Reduce the heat to medium. Sauté the onion, celery, and carrot until soft, 3 to 5 minutes. Add the roasted peppers, garlic, jalapeños, chile powder, cumin, oregano, and cinnamon. Cook until fragrant, about 2 minutes.

3. Add the stewed tomatoes with their juice, reserved chicken, chicken broth, beans, corn, masa, sugar (if using), bay leaves, and chipotle. Bring to a boil, and reduce the heat to medium-low. Simmer, covered slightly, for 40 minutes, stirring occasionally. Discard bay leaves.

4. Taste and adjust the seasoning if necessary. Add the cilantro and lime juice to the pot and stir to combine. Garnish with chopped cilantro, sour cream, lime wedges, and grated cheeses. Serve with cornbread.

Roasted Peppers and Garlic

Skillet-roasting peppers and garlic, and sometimes onions, too, is a traditional Mexican technique that I've adopted for this chili recipe. You can use the basic instructions anytime you need roasted peppers, or use a broiler or stovetop flame.

Roasting Peppers: Place the whole peppers in a skillet or heavy cast-iron griddle over medium-high heat, and turn them occasionally until they are black and charred on all sides, about 10 minutes. Remove from the pan, place in a bowl, and cover with a plate, allowing the peppers to sweat for about 20 minutes. Then peel, seed, and chop the peppers.

Alternatively, roast the peppers directly on the open flame of a conventional gas-stove element, or under a broiler. Turn them occasionally until they are charred on all sides, then place them in a bowl and cover for 20 minutes. Peel, seed, and chop the peppers.

Roasting Garlic: Prick the unpeeled cloves so that they don't explode. Place the cloves in a skillet or heavy cast-iron griddle over medium heat, and turn them occasionally until they are slightly charred on all sides and soft inside, 6 to 7 minutes. Cool and peel.

Note: Jars of roasted red peppers can also be purchased at most supermarkets or specialty food stores.

1 tablespoon masa cornmeal (see note, page 52)

2 teaspoons sugar, optional

2 bay leaves

1 chipotle chile in adobo sauce, chopped (see note, page 13)

1/2 cup chopped fresh cilantro, plus additional for garnish

Freshly squeezed juice of 1/2 lime, plus additional lime wedges for garnish

Sour cream

Grated Monterey Jack and Cheddar cheeses

Ma Duke's Chili
(From my mom, Angela Smith)

2 tablespoons canola oil

1 pound ground turkey

Kosher salt and freshly
    ground black pepper

1 cup chopped onions

1 cup chopped green bell
    pepper

3 garlic cloves, chopped

3 tablespoons mild chili
    powder

2 tablespoons ground cumin

1 tablespoon ground coriander

1 teaspoon dried oregano

2 bay leaves

4 cups low-sodium chicken
    broth or stock

2 (15-ounce) cans stewed
    tomatoes, with juice

1 (15-ounce) can black beans,
    rinsed and drained

1 (15-ounce) can pinto beans,
    rinsed and drained

1 (6-ounce) can tomato paste

2 chipotle peppers in adobo
    sauce, finely chopped (see
    note, page 13)

2 teaspoons dark brown sugar

1 tablespoon masa cornmeal
    (see note)

Freshly squeezed juice of 1/2
    lime, or to taste

1/2 cup chopped fresh cilantro

My mom made this chili about once a week, 'cause we all loved it. With all the spices in this chili, you don't miss the beef at all. The masa cornmeal adds a hint of corn flavor and also thickens it. This chili tastes even better when made a day in advance, but don't add the lime juice and cilantro until just before serving. Serve this with cornbread. **Makes 8 servings**

1. Heat a large Dutch oven over high heat for a few minutes, then add the oil and let warm. Add the ground turkey, season with salt and pepper, and cook, breaking up large pieces with a spoon, until the meat is well-browned, about 5 minutes.

2. Reduce the heat to medium-high. Add the onions and green pepper, and cook, stirring, until the onions are translucent, 4 to 6 minutes.

3. Add the garlic, chili powder, cumin, coriander, oregano, and bay leaves, and cook, stirring, until fragrant, about 30 seconds. Stir in the chicken broth, tomatoes with their juice, beans, tomato paste, chipotles, and brown sugar.

4. Bring the liquid to a boil. Sprinkle the masa over the chili and stir well. Reduce the heat to medium-low, partially cover the pot, and simmer, stirring occasionally, for 1 hour. Discard bay leaves.

5. Taste and add salt and pepper if needed. Season with lime juice to taste, and garnish with the cilantro.

Note: Masa Cornmeal Masa harina, Spanish for "dough flour," is a dried and ground corn flour used in Mexican tortillas and tamales. It can be reconstituted in water to make the standard cornmeal dough, and also works well as a thickener when added straight into soups and stews. Masa harina is available in the ethnic section of most supermarkets, or can be purchased online at www.mexgrocer.com.

Smoked Duck Gumbo

Tony got addicted to gumbo while playing for the Rams. The mother of one of his teammates used to cook up humongous pots of it for the team after every game. This version is rich and elegant, and loaded with pieces of smoked duck breast. I got the idea to add smoked duck breast to gumbo from a restaurant in Baltimore, and now it's Tony's all-time favorite gumbo recipe. It also works with smoked turkey if you can't get smoked duck. **Makes 8 servings**

1. In a Dutch oven over medium-high heat, cook the sausage until slightly browned, 6 to 8 minutes. Use a slotted spoon to transfer the sausage to a paper-towel-lined plate.

2. Reduce the heat to medium. Add the oil, then whisk in the flour until smooth. Cook, stirring constantly with a wooden spoon or rubber spatula, until the roux is the color of chocolate, about 20 minutes.

3. Add the onions, celery, and green pepper, and cook, stirring occasionally, until the vegetables soften, 6 to 8 minutes. Add the garlic, bay leaves, thyme, and cayenne, and cook, stirring, 1 minute more.

4. Stir in the chicken broth and Cajun seasoning, and bring the liquid to a boil. Reduce the heat to medium-low and simmer gently, stirring frequently, for 35 minutes. Skim the surface to remove excess fat. Discard bay leaves.

5. Add the andouille and duck and simmer for 20 minutes more. Stir in the scallions and parsley and serve.

1 pound andouille sausage, cut into 1/4-inch cubes (see note, page 47)

1/2 cup canola oil

1 cup all-purpose flour

2 cups chopped onions

1 cup chopped celery

1 cup chopped green bell pepper

3 garlic cloves, finely chopped

2 bay leaves

1 teaspoon dried thyme

3/4 teaspoon cayenne pepper

6 cups low-sodium chicken broth or stock

1 1/2 teaspoons Cajun seasoning (see note, page 54)

2 pounds smoked duck breast, fat removed, cut into 1/2-inch cubes (see note, page 59)

1/2 cup chopped scallions

1/4 cup chopped fresh flat-leaf parsley

Note: Cajun Seasoning A fiery spice mix with typical Cajun flavors, including thyme and paprika, this seasoning is widely available wherever spices are sold and can be purchased online at www.penzeys.com.

Note: Smoked Duck Breast Meaty and flavorful, smoked duck breast has an intense, rich, smoky flavor, and will keep in the refrigerator for up to 2 months. It is available prepackaged in some specialty food markets. Smoked duck breast can also be easily purchased online from such reputable purveyors as www.dartagnan.com or www.grimaudfarms.com.

Pizzas and Sandwiches

Veggie Pizza

3 tablespoons extra virgin olive oil

1 large Spanish onion, thinly sliced

Kosher salt

2 large portobello mushrooms

1/2 recipe Honey Whole Wheat Crust (recipe follows)

1/4 cup pesto sauce

1/2 cup sliced roasted red bell pepper (see box, page 51)

1/2 cup fresh baby spinach

1/2 cup crumbled goat cheese

1/4 cup freshly grated Parmigiano-Reggiano cheese

Crushed red pepper flakes

1/4 cup finely chopped fresh flat-leaf parsley

I love veggies and I love pizza and I love them together, especially in this recipe, which is heavy on the veggies. The pesto adds a rich, zesty quality and tastes terrific with the veggies. The recipe for the crust makes twice as much as you need. You can freeze the rest. **Makes 6 servings**

1. Preheat the oven to 450° F and heat a baking stone (see note) in the bottom of the oven (on the lowest rack if you have an electric oven) for 1 hour.

2. While the oven is preheating, caramelize the onion. Heat 2 tablespoons of the oil over medium heat. Add the onion and a pinch of salt, and cook, stirring occasionally, until the onion turns golden brown and caramelized, about 40 minutes.

3. Preheat a grill pan or a grill, if desired. Brush the mushrooms with the remaining tablespoon of olive oil and grill until browned on both sides, about 5 minutes per side. Let cool and slice ¼ inch thick.

4. On a floured surface, roll out the pizza dough to form one 12-inch crust. Transfer the crust to the baking stone, and bake for 3 minutes on each side. Transfer the pizza crust to your work surface.

5. Spread the pesto evenly on the crust. Top with the mushrooms, onion, bell pepper, spinach, goat cheese, and Parmigiano-Reggiano, and season lightly with salt and crushed red pepper. Bake until the cheese has melted, 10 to 12 minutes. Sprinkle with parsley and serve immediately.

Honey Whole Wheat Crust

Makes 2 (10- to 12-inch) crusts

1. In a small bowl, stir together the water, honey, and yeast. Let the mixture proof until foamy, about 6 minutes. In the bowl of an electric mixer fitted with the dough hook, mix together the flours and the salt. When the yeast mixture has proofed, add 1 tablespoon of the oil. Pour the yeast mixture over the dry ingredients.

2. Knead the dough on low speed for 10 minutes. The dough will form a ball around the hook when it is ready. Place the dough in a well-oiled bowl, turning to coat evenly. Cover the bowl tightly with plastic wrap and let rise in a warm place until doubled in size, about 2½ hours, depending on the warmth of your kitchen.

3. Once the dough has risen, punch it down. Place it on a baking sheet or Silpat, cover tightly with plastic wrap, and let rise in a warm place for 1 hour more. (The dough can be made up to this point and placed in the refrigerator overnight.)

4. When ready to use, roll the crust out on a floured board and bake according to the recipe directions.

1/2 cup warm water (110° F)

1 tablespoon honey

1 1/8 teaspoons active dry yeast (about half of a 1/4-ounce package)

1 1/4 cups unbleached all-purpose flour

1/2 cup whole wheat flour

1 1/2 teaspoons kosher salt

1 tablespoon extra virgin olive oil, plus additional for greasing the bowl

Note: Baking Stone Available at most kitchen supply stores, baking stones are ideal for turning out crisp, golden-crusted pizzas. Excellent conductors of heat, pizza stones also absorb the moisture released from the dough during baking, resulting in a crust that can stand up to high temperatures without burning. For optimum results, place the stone in the oven at the desired temperature at least 15 minutes prior to baking.

BBQ Chicken Pizza with Cheddar and Monterey Jack

1 cup high-quality prepared barbecue sauce

1 tablespoon minced red onion

2 teaspoons minced garlic

1 teaspoon ground cumin

1 teaspoon chili powder, or to taste

1 teaspoon freshly squeezed lime juice

3 cups roasted, shredded chicken breast

Flour for dusting

1 recipe Honey Whole Wheat Crust (page 57)

Extra virgin olive oil, for brushing

1/3 cup grated sharp white Cheddar cheese

1/3 cup grated Monterey Jack cheese

1/4 cup finely chopped fresh cilantro

One of our favorite pizza places, Wolfgang Puck's, serves a barbecue chicken pizza, and as good as it is there, my version is better. The combination of Cheddar and Monterey Jack, plus plenty of fresh cilantro and lime juice, give this pizza what it's missing at the restaurant. Use your favorite barbecue sauce for this recipe and don't be afraid to make it spicy. **Makes 6 servings**

1. In a small saucepan over medium heat, bring the barbecue sauce, onion, garlic, cumin, chili powder, and lime juice to a boil. Reduce the heat to medium-low, and simmer for 20 minutes.

2. Take the sauce off the heat and stir in the chicken.

3. Heat a baking stone (see note, page 57) in the bottom of a 450° F oven. Divide the pizza dough into two balls, and, on a lightly floured board, roll each crust into a 10-inch circle. Bake each crust for 3 minutes, then flip it and brush the top lightly with olive oil. Bake for another 2 minutes, then transfer the crusts to your work surface.

4. Spread the chicken mixture evenly over the two crusts. Top each crust with half of each cheese. Bake 6 to 8 minutes, until the cheese has melted. Sprinkle each pizza with half of the cilantro. Serve immediately.

✳ Five-Cheese Pizza with Sun-dried Tomato Sauce

Tony and I are cheese fiends. We love everything that includes cheese, from a simple cheese course to homemade macaroni and cheese to pizza with extra cheese. So of course this pizza is just a little slice of heaven for us. The sun-dried tomato sauce gives it a really intense, savory flavor.

Makes 6 servings

1. To make the sauce, heat a medium saucepan over medium-high heat. Add the oil and onion and cook, stirring occasionally, until light brown, 8 to 10 minutes. Add the garlic and sauté for 1 minute more. Reduce the heat to medium-low and add the sun-dried tomatoes, salt, pepper, sugar, oregano, and 1 tablespoon water. Simmer until the sauce has thickened, about 20 minutes.

2. Transfer the sauce to a food processor, add 2 tablespoons of basil, and pulse until slightly pureed but still chunky.

3. Preheat the oven to 450° F and place a baking stone (see note, page 57) on the bottom of the oven, if desired. Place the crust on a baking sheet or directly on the preheated stone and bake for 3 minutes. Transfer the crust to your work surface, and spread ½ cup of the tomato sauce evenly onto the crust. Sprinkle the cheeses evenly over the sauce. Season lightly with salt and pepper, and bake the pizza until the cheese has melted, 6 to 8 minutes. Sprinkle with the basil and serve immediately.

For the sun-dried tomato sauce:

1/2 teaspoon extra virgin olive oil

1/4 cup minced red onion

3/4 teaspoon minced garlic

1 1/2 cups oil-packed sun-dried tomatoes, drained

3/4 teaspoon kosher salt

1/4 teaspoon freshly ground black pepper

1/4 teaspoon sugar

1/4 teaspoon dried oregano

2 tablespoons chopped fresh basil

1 large store-bought pizza crust (such as Boboli)

1/4 cup thinly sliced fresh mozzarella

1/4 cup grated Fontina cheese

1/4 cup crumbled goat cheese

1 tablespoon grated Parmigiano-Reggiano cheese

1 tablespoon grated pecorino Romano cheese

Kosher salt and freshly ground black pepper

1/4 cup fresh basil, cut into a chiffonade (see note, page 32)

Turkey Club and Avocado Wrap

4 (10-inch) whole wheat tortillas, warmed

1/2 pound thinly sliced smoked turkey, preferably peppered

8 slices bacon, chopped and cooked

1 cup fresh baby spinach

1 cup diced Hass avocado

1 cup diced roasted red bell pepper (see box, page 51)

3 tablespoons chopped fresh flat-leaf parsley

1 teaspoon freshly squeezed lime juice

Kosher salt and freshly ground black pepper

Stuffed with turkey, bacon, roasted peppers, and avocado, this is the wrap version of a turkey club. But it's a great alternative to the sandwich because it doesn't fill you up as much. Growing up in California, Tony ate avocados for breakfast, lunch, and dinner, so I use plenty in this wrap.

Makes 4 servings

1. To assemble the wraps, place the tortillas in a row. Place a quarter of the turkey, bacon, spinach, avocado, red pepper, and parsley along the bottom half of each tortilla. Sprinkle some lime juice over each, and season with salt and pepper.

2. Fold the sides of each tortilla slightly over the filling toward the center. Fold the bottom edge toward the center, away from you, then roll gently until the tortilla is completely wrapped around the filling.

Chicken Caesar Wrap

This is Tony's favorite salad made into a wrap. I used to pick these up for Tony from a gourmet market when we lived in St. Louis. When the market closed, I started making them myself. **Makes 4 servings**

1. Combine the dressing ingredients in a blender and blend until smooth. Taste and adjust the seasoning if necessary.

2. Place the lettuce, chicken, croutons, cheese, and half of the dressing in a large bowl, and toss to coat. If necessary, add more dressing, 1 tablespoon at a time.

3. To assemble the wraps, spread a quarter of the salad along the bottom half of each tortilla. Fold the sides slightly over the filling toward the center. Fold the bottom edge toward the center, away from you, and roll gently until the tortilla is completely wrapped around the filling.

For the Caesar dressing:

1/3 cup freshly squeezed lemon juice

1/4 cup extra virgin olive oil

2 tablespoons grated Parmigiano-Reggiano cheese

1 tablespoon Dijon mustard

1 tablespoon Worcestershire sauce

1 to 2 teaspoons honey, to taste

1 teaspoon hot sauce

3 anchovy fillets

2 garlic cloves

Kosher salt and freshly ground black pepper

4 cups chopped romaine lettuce leaves (about 4 romaine hearts)

1 pound roasted chicken breast, pulled

1/2 cup homemade croutons (page 27), cut into 1/2-inch cubes

2 tablespoons grated Parmigiano-Reggiano cheese

4 (10-inch) spinach or sun-dried tomato tortillas, warmed

# Reuben Melt

For the Russian dressing:

3/4 cup low-fat or regular mayonnaise

1/4 cup ketchup

2 tablespoons capers, rinsed and finely chopped

1 tablespoon finely chopped fresh flat-leaf parsley

1 teaspoon grated red onion

1 teaspoon Worcestershire sauce

1 teaspoon hot sauce

6 slices rye bread

Unsalted butter

1¼ pounds thinly sliced corned beef brisket

1¼ cups warm sauerkraut, well-drained

6 slices Gruyère cheese

I didn't think I liked Reuben sandwiches until Tony and I lived in Baltimore when he was playing for the Ravens. He used to order them all the time, and finally I tried a bite. I was instantly converted. I especially love this version, which uses homemade Russian dressing. It's the bomb. You can cook these on a griddle, but if you're making them for a crowd it's easier to bake them in the oven. **Makes 6 servings**

1. To make the Russian dressing, in a blender combine the mayonnaise, ketchup, capers, parsley, onion, Worcestershire sauce, and hot sauce, and blend until smooth.

2. Preheat the oven to 400° F. Spread the butter on one side of each slice of bread. Flip the bread and spread each slice with 1 tablespoon of dressing. Divide the corned beef and sauerkraut evenly among the bread slices and top each with a slice of cheese.

3. Arrange the sandwiches, butter side down, on a foil-lined baking sheet. Bake 5 to 7 minutes, until the cheese is golden and bubbly. Serve hot.

Herbed Turkey Cheeseburger with Bacon and Chipotle Mayo

Tony doesn't think a burger is a burger without bacon. There are many dry turkey burgers out there, but this isn't one of them. **Makes 4 servings**

1. In a large bowl, combine the turkey, cilantro, parsley, garlic powder, Spanish seasoning, and black pepper, and mix well. Divide the mixture into 4 equal portions, shaping each portion into a 3/4-inch-thick patty. (The burgers can be made ahead and frozen in resealable plastic bags, separated by layers of wax paper, for up to 1 month. To defrost, transfer the bag to the refrigerator and thaw overnight.)

2. Heat a grill or broiler to high heat. If using a broiler, place the rack in the upper third of the oven. Brush both sides of the patties with oil, and grill or broil until just cooked through, about 4 minutes per side. Turn off the heat, and top with the cheese.

3. While the burgers cook, in a small bowl, stir together all the ingredients for the chipotle mayonnaise.

4. To assemble the burgers, spread the top and bottom of each bun with chipotle mayo. Add to each bun a burger, 2 slices of bacon, a slice of tomato, and a lettuce leaf. Serve immediately.

1 1/2 pounds ground turkey

2 tablespoons finely chopped fresh cilantro

2 tablespoons finely chopped fresh flat-leaf parsley

2 teaspoons garlic powder

1 teaspoon all-purpose Spanish seasoning (such as Goya seasoning)

1/4 teaspoon freshly ground black pepper

1 teaspoon canola oil

4 slices Monterey Jack cheese

4 whole wheat hamburger buns, toasted

8 slices thick-sliced bacon, cooked

4 slices tomato

4 curly-leaf lettuce leaves

For the chipotle mayonnaise:

1/2 cup low-fat mayonnaise

2 teaspoons adobo sauce from canned chipotle peppers (see note, page 13)

1 teaspoon freshly squeezed lime juice

Pinch of kosher salt

Asian Tuna Steak Sandwiches

For the cucumber salad:

2 tablespoons chopped scallions

2 tablespoons finely chopped fresh cilantro

2 tablespoons rice wine vinegar

1 tablespoon Thai or Vietnamese fish sauce (see note, page 37)

1 tablespoon sugar

1 teaspoon minced ginger

1 teaspoon minced garlic

1 teaspoon Thai chili paste (see note, page 23)

1 teaspoon sesame oil

1 large cucumber, peeled, halved lengthwise, seeds scraped out, thinly sliced

For the wasabi mayo:

1/4 cup low-fat mayonnaise

2 teaspoons finely chopped fresh cilantro

1 teaspooon low-sodium soy sauce

1/2 teaspoon wasabi powder

4 (6-ounce) sushi-grade tuna steaks (see note)

2 teaspoons canola oil

Kosher salt and freshly ground black pepper

4 kaiser rolls, split and toasted

1 cup daikon radish sprouts

This is my fantasy of what a tuna sandwich would taste like if you ordered it from a sushi restaurant: spicy from the wasabi mayo, crunchy from the ginger-cucumber salad, and, of course, sweet and melt-in-the-mouth tender from great-quality tuna. When it comes to tuna sandwiches, this is as gourmet as it gets. **Makes 4 servings**

1. To make the cucumber salad, in a medium bowl, whisk together the scallions, cilantro, vinegar, fish sauce, sugar, ginger, garlic, chili paste, and sesame oil. Add the cucumber, toss to coat, and let stand at room temperature for at least 1 hour. Drain and set aside.

2. In a small bowl, stir together all the ingredients for the wasabi mayo.

3. Heat a grill or a nonstick skillet over medium-high heat until very hot. Brush both sides of each tuna steak with oil, and season with salt and pepper. Sear the tuna, turning once, until the edges are cooked but the center remains rare, 2 to 3 minutes on each side.

4. To assemble the sandwiches, spread the top and bottom of each roll with the mayonnaise. Divide the daikon sprouts evenly among the bottoms. Add the tuna steaks, and top each sandwich with a quarter of the cucumber salad. Cover with the tops and serve immediately.

Note: Sushi-Grade Tuna Bright red in color and rich in flavor, sushi-grade tuna usually refers to tuna that has been flash-frozen within hours of being caught. Because tuna is at its most flavorful eaten raw to medium-rare, procuring fish that is as fresh as possible is an excellent way to minimize the risk of food-borne illness. Sushi-grade tuna can be purchased at some seafood markets, or ordered online at www.pikeplacefish.com.

Fish Tacos with Mango Salsa

There are as many fish-taco stands in San Diego, where Tony grew up, as there are gas stations. This is my version of that street-food favorite, which I make without the usual creamy white sauce. Instead, I add mango salsa, which I love for its sweet-spicy juiciness, and in place of the raw cabbage found in most fish tacos, I like to use pickled red cabbage for its salty tang. **Makes 4 servings**

1. In a medium bowl, stir together the salsa ingredients. Taste and adjust the seasoning if necessary. Cover tightly with plastic wrap and let stand at room temperature for at least 30 minutes or up to 4 hours.

2. Season both sides of the fish with cumin, salt, and pepper. Brush both sides with oil. Heat a grill or a grill pan over medium-high heat until hot but not smoking. Grill the fish, turning once, until just opaque in the center but not flaking, about 4 minutes on each side. Transfer the fish to a cutting board and cut into chunks.

3. While the fish is cooking, heat the corn tortillas on the grill until hot, about 30 seconds on each side. Transfer each tortilla to a plate and stack between layers of aluminum foil to keep warm.

4. Divide the fish chunks among the 8 tortillas. Top each tortilla with ¼ cup of the red cabbage and ¼ cup of the mango salsa. Squeeze lime juice over each taco and serve hot.

For the mango salsa:

1/2 cup finely diced mango

1/2 cup finely diced red bell pepper

1/4 cup finely diced red onion

1/2 serrano chile pepper, finely chopped

2 tablespoons finely chopped fresh cilantro

1 tablespoon freshly squeezed lime juice

1 teaspoon honey

1/4 teaspoon kosher salt

1 pound red snapper fillets

1 teaspoon ground cumin

Kosher salt and freshly ground black pepper

1 teaspoon extra virgin olive oil

8 (6-inch) corn tortillas

2 cups "Pickled" Red Cabbage (see page 139) or shredded raw red cabbage

2 lime wedges

Mediterranean Panini with Prosciutto and Tapenade

1 large portobello mushroom

Extra virgin olive oil, for brushing

8 slices Italian bread

4 tablespoons black-olive tapenade

12 slices buffalo mozzarella

8 thin slices prosciutto

2 roasted red peppers, well-drained, cut in half (see box, page 51)

8 fresh basil leaves

Kosher salt and freshly ground black pepper

I know you've seen prosciutto everywhere in this book, because it is probably one of my favorite ingredients on the planet. It's excellent in this sandwich, paired with tapenade, roasted red peppers, and mozzarella. **Makes 4 servings**

1. Heat a grill or nonstick griddle over high heat. Brush the mushroom cap generously with olive oil. Grill the mushroom, adding more oil if necessary, until it is cooked through and most of its juice has evaporated, about 5 minutes on each side. Turn off the heat and transfer the mushroom to a cutting board. Slice the mushroom into ¼-inch strips. Reduce the heat of the grill or griddle to medium-high.

2. To assemble the sandwiches, place the bread slices in a row. Spread ½ tablespoon of tapenade over each slice. Top 4 slices of bread with 3 slices of mozzarella, 2 slices of prosciutto, a quarter of the mushroom slices, a red pepper half, and 2 basil leaves. Season lightly with salt and pepper, and add the top layer of bread, pressing to compress gently.

3. Brush the tops of the sandwiches with olive oil and lay them on the grill, oil side down. Brush the tops of the sandwiches with olive oil. Weight each sandwich down, using a foil-covered brick or heavy cast-iron skillet. Cook the sandwiches until golden, about 2 minutes per side, making sure the sandwiches are weighted down the entire time. Serve hot.

Pastas and Risotto

Pasta Pomodoro

2 tablespoons extra virgin
  olive oil

3 garlic cloves, minced

3 cups canned crushed
  tomatoes, about
  2 (15-ounce) cans

2 teaspoons sugar, or to taste,
  optional

1/4 teaspoon crushed red
  pepper flakes

Kosher salt and freshly
  ground black pepper

1 pound spaghetti

8 fresh basil leaves, cut into
  a chiffonade (see note,
  page 32)

Simple and delicious, this classic pasta dish is another quick and easy meal that can be ready in minutes. The sauce tastes better if made a day or so in advance; just reheat it as the pasta cooks. **Makes 4 servings**

1. Heat the oil in a large skillet over medium heat. Add the garlic and cook until it begins to brown, 1 to 2 minutes. Add the tomatoes, sugar (if using), crushed red pepper, and salt and pepper to taste, and bring to a boil. Reduce the heat to medium-low and cook, uncovered, until the sauce thickens, about 20 minutes. Taste and adjust the seasoning if necessary. If not using immediately, let cool completely, then refrigerate until needed, up to 5 days.

2. While the sauce cooks, bring a large pot of salted water to a boil. Add the spaghetti and cook until the pasta is al dente, 6 to 8 minutes. Drain well and reserve 1 cup of the cooking water.

3. Add the cooked pasta and the basil to the skillet with the sauce and toss to coat. If the pasta seems dry, add some of the pasta cooking water, 1 tablespoon at a time, and toss to combine. Serve immediately.

Linguine alla Puttanesca

Tony loves anchovies and the complex flavor they give to this traditional Italian dish. I love pasta in general, and the fact that this recipe can be on the table in 30 minutes. So it's a winner in both of our books. **Makes 4 servings**

1. Heat the oil in a large skillet over medium heat. Add the garlic and sauté until it begins to brown, about 3 minutes. Add the anchovies, oregano, and crushed red pepper, and cook until fragrant, about 15 seconds. Add the tomatoes, olives, and capers, and bring to a boil. Reduce the heat to medium-low and cook, uncovered, until the sauce thickens, 15 to 20 minutes. Add salt and pepper to taste. Once cooked, cover the sauce if necessary to keep warm, or warm it up just before serving.

2. While the sauce is simmering, bring a large pot of salted water to a boil. Add the linguine, and cook until the pasta is al dente, 6 to 8 minutes. Drain well, and reserve 1 cup of the cooking water.

3. Add the cooked pasta and parsley to the skillet with the sauce, turn the heat to low, and toss well. If the sauce is too thick, add some of the pasta cooking water, 1 tablespoon at a time, and toss again, repeating until the sauce reaches the desired consistency and coats the pasta. Transfer the pasta to a large bowl, top with the cheese, and serve.

2 tablespoons extra virgin olive oil

4 garlic cloves, thinly sliced

2 anchovy fillets, chopped

1 teaspoon dried oregano

1/4 teaspoon crushed red pepper flakes

3 cups canned crushed tomatoes, about 2 (15 ounce) cans

1/2 cup Kalamata olives, pitted and sliced

2 tablespoons capers, rinsed and drained

Kosher salt and freshly ground black pepper

1 pound linguine

1/4 cup chopped fresh flat-leaf parsley

2 tablespoons grated Parmigiano-Reggiano cheese

Black Pasta with Creamy Tomato and Shrimp Sauce

2 tablespoons extra virgin
olive oil

1/4 cup minced shallot

2 garlic cloves, minced

1/2 teaspoon crushed red
pepper flakes

1 pound large shrimp, peeled
and deveined (see note,
page 20)

1 (15-ounce) can crushed
tomatoes

1/4 cup dry white wine

1/2 teaspoon kosher salt

1 pound black (squid ink)
pasta, or other pasta

1/4 cup heavy cream

1/4 cup chopped fresh flat-leaf
parsley

Squid-ink pasta is one of those gourmet items from the eighties that stand the test of time. I love the way it looks, very dark and dramatic with the pink shrimp sauce on top. But, since it doesn't have a flavor that's much different from regular pasta, you can substitute that here, though you'll lose points in the presentation. **Makes 4 servings**

1. Heat the oil in a large skillet over medium-high heat. Add the shallot and garlic and cook, stirring constantly, for about 1 minute. Add the crushed red pepper and shrimp, and cook for 1 minute more. Transfer the shrimp to a plate and cover to keep warm.

2. Add the tomatoes, wine, and salt to the skillet, and bring to a boil. Reduce the heat to medium-low and cook the sauce, uncovered, until thickened, 15 to 20 minutes. Taste and adjust the seasoning if necessary.

3. Meanwhile, bring a large pot of salted water to a boil and add the pasta. Cook until al dente, 6 to 8 minutes. Drain well and reserve 1 cup of the cooking water.

4. Return the shrimp to the skillet and raise the heat to medium-high. Add the cream and toss to coat. Add the pasta and parsley, and toss well. If the sauce is too thick, add some of the pasta cooking water, 1 tablespoon at a time, until the sauce reaches the desired consistency and coats the pasta. Serve immediately.

Cajun Seafood Pasta

My friend's mom was the inspiration for this dish. She's from Baton Rouge, and she can really cook! Chock-full of shrimp and crab coated in a superspicy, creamy sauce, it's so hearty and filling, Tony doesn't even miss the meat.

Makes 4 servings

1. In a large skillet over medium heat, melt the butter. Add the flour, whisking constantly, and cook until smooth and slightly thickened, about 3 minutes.

2. Add the onion, celery, and peppers, and sauté until soft, about 8 minutes. Add the milk, garlic, Cajun seasoning, cayenne, and thyme, and bring to a boil. Reduce the heat to medium-low, then add the hot sauce and Worcestershire sauce. Cook until the sauce coats the back of a spoon, about 7 minutes. You can prepare the sauce up to this point several hours ahead (store it in the refrigerator if you want to make it a day ahead, then reheat it while you boil the pasta).

3. Bring a large pot of salted water to a boil. Add the pasta and cook until al dente, 6 to 8 minutes. Drain well and reserve 1 cup of the cooking water.

4. Gently stir the crabmeat and shrimp into the sauce and cook for 1 minute. If the sauce is too thick, add some of the pasta cooking water, 1 tablespoon at a time, until the sauce reaches the desired consistency. Add the pasta, scallions, and parsley, and toss to combine. Taste and adjust the seasoning if necessary. Serve immediately.

3 tablespoons unsalted butter

3 tablespoons all-purpose flour

1/2 cup finely chopped onion

1/4 cup finely chopped celery

1/4 cup finely chopped green bell pepper

1/4 cup finely chopped red bell pepper

2 cups whole milk

2 tablespoons minced garlic

2 teaspoons Cajun seasoning (see note, page 54)

1 teaspoon cayenne pepper

1 teaspoon dried thyme

2 teaspoons hot sauce

1 teaspoon Worcestershire sauce

1 pound fettuccine

1/2 pound lump crabmeat, picked clean (see note, page 19)

1/2 pound large shrimp, cut in half lengthwise, peeled and deveined (see note, page 20)

1/2 cup finely chopped scallions

1/4 cup finely chopped fresh flat-leaf parsley

Kosher salt and freshly ground black pepper

Linguine with Fresh Tomatoes and Clams

1 tablespoon extra virgin olive oil

3 garlic cloves, thinly sliced

1/2 teaspoon crushed red pepper flakes

4 dozen littleneck clams, scrubbed

2 cups diced tomatoes

2/3 cup dry white wine

1/2 cup low-sodium chicken broth or stock

1 pound linguine

1 tablespoon freshly squeezed lemon juice

1/2 cup chopped fresh flat-leaf parsley

1/4 teaspoon kosher salt

1/4 cup freshly grated Parmigiano-Reggiano cheese

The secret to a great linguine with clam sauce is using plenty of fresh clams. Here I combine them with diced ripe tomatoes, white wine, and herbs for a fresh-tasting take on the usual recipe. I got the inspiration from one of our favorite restaurants in Houston, which serves the best clam sauce ever! Their dish is so good that Tony didn't like linguine with clam sauce at all until he tasted theirs. **Makes 4 servings**

1. Heat the oil in a large saucepan over medium-high heat. Add the garlic and crushed red pepper and cook for 1 minute.

2. Add the clams, tomatoes, wine, and broth, and bring to a boil. Cover and reduce the heat to medium. Cook for 5 minutes, then check the clams to see if they've opened. Transfer the clams to a bowl as they open, allowing about 15 minutes for all of them to open. Discard any unopened clams.

3. Bring a large pot of salted water to a boil. Add the linguine and cook, until al dente, 6 to 8 minutes. Drain well.

4. Cook the sauce over medium heat until slightly thickened, 7 to 10 minutes. Meanwhile, pull the clam meat from the shells, if desired. Return the clams to the pan. Add the pasta, lemon juice, parsley, and salt and cook for 2 minutes. Taste and adjust the seasoning if necessary. Serve at once, with the cheese on the side.

✳ Seafood Lasagna

This is a delicate, creamy lasagna that's perfect for a fancy dinner party because of the lobster meat. Tony absolutely loves this dish. If you don't feel like splurging for lobster, you can substitute diced cooked shrimp. You'll notice I don't cook the pasta before assembling the lasagna. Because I use fresh pasta here, it works! **Makes 8 servings**

1. Preheat the oven to 350° F. In a medium saucepan over medium heat, melt the butter. Whisk in the flour and cook until smooth and slightly thickened, about 3 minutes. Slowly whisk in the milk, salt, pepper, and nutmeg. Cook, stirring constantly, until the sauce coats the back of a spoon, 4 to 6 minutes. Taste and adjust the seasoning.

2. Remove the sauce from the heat and stir in the spinach and ½ cup of the Parmigiano-Reggiano cheese.

3. In a medium bowl, combine the ricotta, mozzarella, egg, basil, parsley, and garlic. Season with salt and pepper to taste. (Don't add too much salt, as the cheese tends to be a little salty.) Mix well.

4. In a medium bowl, combine the lobster meat and crabmeat and season lightly with salt and pepper.

5. To assemble, spread 1 cup of the sauce on the bottom of a 13 X 9-inch baking dish. Cover with pasta. Spread ¼ of the cheese mixture over the pasta. Top with ¼ of the crab mixture. Pour 1 cup of sauce on top. Repeat the layers until all the ingredients are used, ending with the sauce. (Reserve extra sauce, if possible, for future use.) Sprinkle the remaining ¼ cup of Parmigiano-Reggiano on top.

6. Bake, uncovered, 25 to 30 minutes, until golden and bubbly. Let stand 10 minutes before cutting.

Note: You'll need about 3 lobsters or lobster tails to yield 1½ pounds cooked lobster meat.

---

4 tablespoons (1/2 stick) unsalted butter

1/4 cup all-purpose flour

31/2 cups whole milk

11/2 teaspoons kosher salt, plus additional

1/2 teaspoon freshly ground black pepper, plus additional

Pinch of freshly grated nutmeg

1/2 pound fresh baby spinach, roughly chopped (about 8 cups)

3/4 cup grated Parmigiano-Reggiano cheese

2 cups ricotta cheese

1 cup shredded part-skim or whole-milk mozzarella cheese

1 large egg

1/4 cup fresh basil, cut into a chiffonade (see note, page 32)

1/4 cup chopped fresh flat-leaf parsley

2 teaspoons chopped garlic

11/2 pounds cooked lobster meat, diced (see note)

3/4 pound lump crabmeat, picked clean (see note, page 19)

1/2 pound fresh lasagna sheets or wonton skins

Spaghetti and Meatballs

For the marinara sauce:

1/4 cup extra virgin olive oil

1 head garlic, cloves separated, peeled, and thinly sliced

2 tablespoons dried oregano

1 teaspoon crushed red pepper flakes

3 bay leaves

4 (28-ounce) cans crushed Italian plum tomatoes

1/2 bottle dry red wine

2 tablespoons sugar, or to taste, optional

1 tablespoon kosher salt

Freshly ground black pepper

1 bunch basil leaves, cut into a chiffonade (see note, page 32)

For the meatballs and pasta:

1/2 pound ground beef chuck

1/2 pound ground veal

1/2 pound ground pork

1/4 cup minced shallot

1/4 cup finely chopped fresh flat-leaf parsley

1/4 cup dried bread crumbs

2 large eggs, lightly beaten

3 tablespoons grated pecorino Romano cheese, plus additional for garnish

3 tablespoons grated Parmigiano-Reggiano cheese, plus additional for garnish

1 tablespoon minced garlic

2 teaspoons kosher salt

When I was in high school, every Sunday the mother of an Italian friend of mine made "gravy." This is my version, and, calling for a whole head of garlic and simmering for hours, it is definitely a Sunday dish. I serve it with Tony's favorite meatballs. He loves "meat-meat," so when I combine three different meats and serve it to him, he's like a kid in a candy store. You may think garlic cheese bread is overkill with the pasta, but, trust me, if you serve it to a group of hungry football players, it will disappear in no time. **Makes 6 servings**

1. To make the sauce, place a large Dutch oven over medium heat and warm the oil. Add the garlic and cook, stirring constantly, until it begins to brown, about 3 minutes. Add the oregano, crushed red pepper, and bay leaves, and cook for 30 seconds.

2. Stir in the tomatoes, wine, sugar (if using), salt, and pepper, and bring to a boil. Reduce the heat to medium-low and simmer, uncovered, for about 2 hours, stirring occasionally. Taste and adjust the seasoning if necessary. (The sauce tastes better the next day, as the acidity of the tomatoes has a chance to mellow. Cool completely and refrigerate, then reheat before serving.) Add the basil just before serving.

3. To make the meatballs, in a large bowl, combine the ground meats, shallot, parsley, bread crumbs, eggs, both cheeses, garlic, salt, oregano, thyme, crushed red pepper, and ground black pepper, and mix well. Gently roll the meat mixture into balls slightly larger than golf balls (you should have 18 to 20 meatballs). Place on a large parchment-lined baking sheet and refrigerate, covered tightly with plastic wrap, for at least 1 hour or up to 24 hours.

4. Place a large nonstick skillet over medium-high heat and add 1/4 cup of the oil. Heat the oil until it is hot but not smoking. Add about half of the meatballs, making sure not to overcrowd the pan, and cook, gently turning them occasionally, until they are well-browned on all sides, 8 to 10 minutes. Transfer the meatballs to a paper-towel-lined plate. Drain the oil and wipe out the skillet. Repeat with the remaining oil and meatballs.

5. Drain and wipe out the skillet again. Return all the meatballs to the skillet and pour enough marinara sauce over them to cover. Bring the sauce to a boil, then reduce the heat to low, and cook, covered, until the meatballs are cooked through, 20 to 30 minutes. (Meatballs and sauce can be stored in the refrigerator for up to 3 days or frozen for up to 1 1/2 months. The leftover sauce can be stored in the freezer for up to 2 months.)

6. Bring a large pot of salted water to a boil. Add the pasta and cook, stirring frequently, until al dente, 6 to 8 minutes. Drain the pasta, place in a large serving bowl, and toss in some of the marinara sauce. Top with several meatballs and more sauce. Garnish with both cheeses.

7. To make the garlic cheese bread, preheat the oven to 350° F. Using a serrated knife, cut the bread in half horizontally. In a small bowl, combine the butter, cheese, parsley, garlic paste, and salt, and mix well. Spread the garlic butter onto both halves of the bread, place the loaf back together, and wrap it tightly in aluminum foil.

8. Bake the loaf in the middle of the oven until heated through, 12 to 15 minutes. Unwrap the foil, place the halves side by side, and cook about 5 minutes more, until lightly browned.

1 teaspoon dried oregano

1/2 teaspoon dried thyme

1/4 teaspoon crushed red pepper flakes

Freshly ground black pepper

1/2 cup extra virgin olive oil

1 pound spaghetti

For the garlic cheese bread:

1 loaf Italian bread

4 tablespoons (1/2 stick) unsalted butter, softened

2 tablespoons freshly grated Parmigiano-Reggiano cheese

1 tablespoon finely chopped fresh flat-leaf parsley

2 teaspoons roasted garlic paste (see box, page 10)

1/4 teaspoon kosher salt

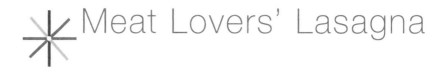

Meat Lovers' Lasagna

1 pound ground beef chuck

1/2 pound ground pork

1/2 pound ground veal

21/2 teaspoons kosher salt

1 teaspoon freshly ground black pepper

1 cup chopped onions

5 garlic cloves, chopped

2 bay leaves

1 tablespoon dried basil

1 tablespoon dried oregano

1 teaspoon crushed red pepper flakes

5 cups canned crushed tomatoes, about 3 (15-ounce) cans

1 (12-ounce) can tomato paste

1 tablespoon sugar

1 pound dried lasagna noodles

2 (15-ounce) containers part-skim or whole-milk ricotta cheese

1/2 cup chopped fresh flat-leaf parsley

1 large egg, lightly beaten

4 cups grated part-skim or whole-milk mozzarella cheese

1/2 cup grated Parmigiano-Reggiano cheese

I remember when my mom used to make meat lasagna; it was always for a special occasion. When I took over the reins, I started making it with three meats—pork for richness, veal for tenderness, and beef for flavor and texture. It's best to make the sauce at least a day ahead (or up to three days ahead). The flavors are better that way, and it's also much easier to assemble the lasagna with cold sauce. **Makes 8 servings**

1. In a large pot over medium-high heat, brown the beef, pork, and veal, breaking up any large chunks, about 7 minutes. Drain off any fat and season with 1 teaspoon of the salt and the black pepper. Add the onions and cook, stirring, until soft, about 5 minutes. Add the garlic, bay leaves, basil, oregano, and crushed red pepper, and cook, stirring constantly, for 1 minute.

2. Stir in the crushed tomatoes, tomato paste, 1 teaspoon of the remaining salt, and the sugar, and bring to a boil. Reduce the heat to medium-low and simmer, uncovered, stirring occasionally, until the sauce has thickened, about 1 1/2 hours. Taste and adjust the seasoning if necessary. Let cool, cover tightly with plastic wrap, and refrigerate until needed, at least 4 hours and up to 3 days.

3. Cook the lasagna noodles according to the package directions and drain. In a small bowl combine the ricotta cheese, parsley, egg, and the remaining 1/2 teaspoon of salt.

4. Preheat the oven to 375° F. To assemble, spoon 1/2 cup of the meat sauce into a 13 X 9-inch baking dish. Cover with a third each of the lasagna noodles, ricotta mixture, mozzarella, and meat sauce. Repeat the layers, ending with the sauce. Sprinkle the Parmigiano-Reggiano cheese evenly over the top. Place the dish on a baking sheet and bake for 45 minutes, until bubbly.

✳ Pad Thai

We love Thai food, and this is our favorite dish. Usually it is served with chicken or shrimp, but I like to serve it with both. The sauce is salty, sour, sweet, and very compelling. Rice stick noodles, made from rice flour and water, are available in Asian markets. In a pinch you could substitute cooked spaghetti (don't soak it), but the texture won't be quite as authentic. **Makes 4 servings**

1. In a large bowl, soak the noodles with warm water to cover until softened, 15 to 20 minutes. Drain the noodles and toss with the sesame oil.

2. In a small bowl, combine the fish sauce, vinegar, honey, and chili paste.

3. Heat a large skillet or wok over medium-high heat for 1 minute, and add the peanut oil. Add the chicken and cook for about 2 minutes. Add the shrimp, garlic, and ginger, and cook for 30 seconds. Transfer to a plate and cover it to keep it warm.

4. Add the eggs to the wok and let them sit for 20 seconds or until they begin to set, then scramble lightly. Add the noodles, chicken and shrimp, sprouts, scallions, and fish-sauce mixture to the wok, and toss to coat. Taste and adjust the seasoning, adding salt if needed.

5. Transfer the noodles to a platter and garnish with the peanuts and cilantro. Squeeze the lime juice over the noodles and serve at once.

Note: Rice Stick Noodles Traditional Thai recipes call for soaking the noodles in warm water until softened, yielding stir-fry-able noodles that are firm and somewhat dry. If you prefer softer, more pastalike noodles, blanch them in boiling water for 5 minutes before stir-frying.

12 ounces rice stick noodles (see note)

1 teaspoon toasted (Asian) sesame oil

2 tablespoons Thai or Vietnamese fish sauce (see note, page 37)

2 tablespoons rice wine vinegar

2 tablespoons honey, or to taste

1 teaspoon Thai chili paste (see note, page 23)

2 tablespoons peanut oil

1/2 pound ground chicken

1/2 pound large shrimp, cut in half lengthwise, peeled, and deveined (see note, page 20)

2 tablespoons minced garlic

1 tablespoon minced ginger

2 large eggs, lightly beaten

1 1/2 cups mung bean sprouts

2/3 cup thinly sliced scallions

Kosher salt to taste

3 tablespoons chopped roasted, unsalted peanuts

1/4 cup finely chopped fresh cilantro

Freshly squeezed juice of 1 lime

Soba Noodles with Five-Spice Flank Steak

1 pound soba noodles, cooked and rinsed with cold water (see box, page 79)

2 carrots, julienned

1 small red bell pepper, julienned

1 bunch scallions, chopped

1/2 cup finely chopped fresh cilantro

11/2 pounds flank steak

1 tablespoon Chinese five-spice powder

Kosher salt and freshly ground black pepper

Cooking spray

1 teaspoon toasted (Asian) sesame oil

4 garlic cloves, minced

1 tablespoon minced ginger

1 cup low-sodium chicken broth or stock

1/4 cup smooth reduced-fat or regular peanut butter

3 tablespoons low-sodium soy sauce

1 tablespoon Thai or Vietnamese fish sauce (see note, page 37)

1 tablespoon rice wine vinegar

2 teaspoons Thai chili paste (see note, page 23)

Freshly squeezed juice of 1/2 lime

I love Asian noodles, especially soba noodles. They have great texture and flavor and the added bonus of being high in protein. Since Tony is crazy for peanut butter, whether it's in a cookie, a sandwich, or tossed with noodles, he's a huge fan of this dish. **Makes 6 servings**

1. In a large bowl, combine the noodles, carrots, red pepper, scallions, and cilantro, and set aside.

2. Season the steak generously on both sides with five-spice powder, salt, and pepper. Heat a grill pan over medium-high heat until hot, 3 to 5 minutes. Coat the pan with cooking spray, and place the flank steak on the pan. Sear the steak, turning once, until browned, 4 to 5 minutes per side for medium-rare. Transfer the steak to a cutting board and let rest for 5 minutes.

3. Heat a small saucepan over medium heat, and add the sesame oil. Add the garlic and ginger, and cook for 1 minute. Add the chicken broth, peanut butter, soy sauce, fish sauce, vinegar, and chili paste, and stir until smooth. Bring the sauce to a boil, reduce the heat to medium-low, and cook, uncovered, until the sauce has thickened, about 10 minutes. Remove the sauce from the heat and stir in the lime juice.

4. Pour the warm sauce over the noodles and gently toss to combine. Slice the steak on a bias and add it to the noodles. Serve at room temperature.

Cooking Soba Noodles

Japanese noodles made from buckwheat flour, soba noodles become overcooked and sticky if prepared like regular wheat pasta. To prepare soba, add the noodles to a large pot of boiling water, and cook, stirring occasionally, until they just soften, 3 to 4 minutes. Transfer them to a colander immediately and drain, then plunge them into a bowl of ice water, and drain again. Rinse the noodles under cold running water, drain, and refrigerate, covered, until you are ready to use them. Both traditional supermarkets and Asian markets carry soba noodles, or they can be ordered online at www.asianfoodgrocer.com.

Wild Mushroom Risotto

Tony loves wild mushrooms and he loves the richness and creaminess of risotto. So this is a no-brainer. **Makes 6 servings**

1. In a medium saucepan over medium heat, bring the broth to a simmer. Reduce the heat to low and keep warm.

2. Heat the oil in a large saucepan over medium heat. Add the shallot and garlic and cook, stirring occasionally, until soft, about 3 minutes. Add the mushrooms and sauté until lightly browned, 5 to 7 minutes. Add the rice and stir to coat.

3. Add the wine, thyme, and bay leaf, and cook, stirring constantly, until the liquid is almost absorbed, 2 to 3 minutes. Begin adding the warm broth, ½ cup at a time, stirring frequently, making sure each portion is absorbed before adding the next. After 20 minutes, check the rice for doneness. It should be tender with a slight crunch.

4. Remove from the heat and discard the bay leaf and thyme sprigs. Add the cheese, parsley, and butter, and stir to combine. Taste and adjust the seasoning if necessary. Serve immediately.

4 cups low-sodium chicken broth or stock

2 tablespoons extra virgin olive oil

1 small shallot, finely chopped

2 garlic cloves, minced

1/2 pound shiitake mushrooms, sliced

1/2 pound cremini mushrooms, sliced

1 1/2 cups Arborio rice (see note, page 80)

1/2 cup dry white wine

4 sprigs fresh thyme

1 bay leaf

1/4 cup grated Parmigiano-Reggiano cheese

1/4 cup chopped fresh flat-leaf parsley

2 tablespoons unsalted butter

Kosher salt and freshly ground black pepper

Asparagus and Sugar Snap Pea Risotto

4 cups low-sodium chicken broth or stock

1 1/2 tablespoons extra virgin olive oil

1/2 cup finely chopped shallot

2 garlic cloves, finely chopped

1 1/2 cups Arborio rice (see note)

1/2 cup dry white wine

2 sprigs fresh thyme

1 bay leaf

Finely grated zest and freshly squeezed juice of 1 lemon

1 1/2 cups fresh or frozen sugar snap peas, thawed, cut in half diagonally

1 1/2 cups fresh asparagus, cut diagonally into 1-inch pieces

1/4 cup freshly grated Parmigiano-Reggiano cheese

Kosher salt and freshly ground black pepper

This is a perfect springtime risotto. Even though asparagus is available all year, it's younger and more tender in the spring, which is also when you can get fresh sugar snap peas. These spring veggies cut the richness of the risotto, and the lemon juice wakes up the whole dish. **Makes 6 servings**

1. In a medium saucepan over medium heat, bring the broth to a simmer. Reduce the heat to low and keep warm.

2. Heat the oil in a large saucepan over medium heat. Add the shallot and garlic and cook, stirring occasionally, until soft, about 3 minutes. Add the rice and stir to coat.

3. Add the wine, thyme, bay leaf, and lemon zest, and cook, stirring constantly, until the liquid is almost absorbed, about 3 minutes. Begin adding the warm broth, 1/2 cup at a time, stirring frequently, making sure each portion is absorbed before adding the next. After 15 minutes, stir in the snap peas, asparagus, and ½ cup of broth. Cook until the liquid is absorbed, 8 to 10 minutes. The rice should be tender with a slight crunch.

4. Remove from the heat and discard the bay leaf and thyme sprigs. Stir in the cheese and the lemon juice. Taste and adjust the seasoning if necessary. Serve immediately.

Note: Arborio Rice Arborio rice is an Italian short-grain rice used in the preparation of classic Italian risotto. Unlike many other varieties of rice, Arborio should never be washed before cooking, as it is precisely the high starch content that gives it its characteristic creamy texture. Arborio rice is widely available in supermarkets and specialty food stores.

Superb Seafood

Blue Corn–Crusted Snapper with Tropical-Fruit Salsa

Sesame-Crusted Mahi-Mahi

Halibut with Spicy Soy Broth

Whole Trout en Papillote with Lemon-Shallot Butter

Blackened Catfish

Asian Salmon with Ginger and Soy

Baked Rockfish with Crab Imperial

Shrimp Creole

Crawfish Étouffée

Cajun-Style King Crab Legs

Deep-Fried Lobster Tails

Blue Corn–Crusted Snapper
with Tropical-Fruit Salsa

For the tropical-fruit salsa:

1 cup diced fresh pineapple

1 cup diced fresh mango

1/2 cup diced red bell pepper

1/4 cup diced red onion

1/4 cup finely chopped fresh cilantro

1 serrano chile pepper, minced

Freshly squeezed juice of 1 lime

2 tablespoons extra virgin olive oil

Kosher salt

4 (8-ounce) red snapper fillets

Kosher salt and freshly ground black pepper

Garlic powder

Ground cumin

1/4 cup all-purpose flour

1 large egg

1 tablespoon milk

1/4 cup blue cornmeal (see note)

3 tablespoons canola oil

I think blue cornmeal has an earthier, deeper flavor than the regular yellow, and I love the way it tastes with sweet red snapper. The spices on the fish make it tasty enough to serve on its own with a squeeze of lemon or lime, but the tropical-fruit salsa adds a welcome juicy kick. Serve this with Cumin Rice (page 149) and Strawberry Daiquiris (see sidebar).

Makes 4 servings

1. To make the salsa, in a medium bowl, combine all the ingredients and mix well. Taste and adjust the seasoning if necessary. Cover tightly with plastic wrap and set aside to marinate for at least 1 hour.

2. Score the skin side of the snapper fillets and season with salt, pepper, garlic powder, and cumin. Mix the flour and a large pinch of salt and pepper in a shallow dish. In a separate shallow dish, whisk together the egg and milk. Mix the cornmeal with another pinch of salt and pepper in a third shallow dish.

3. Dredge each fillet, flesh side down, first in the flour, shaking off the excess, next in the egg mixture, and finally in the cornmeal, pressing on it so it adheres. Don't dredge the skin side of the fish.

4. In a large nonstick skillet over medium-high heat, warm the canola oil until it is hot but not smoking. Add the snapper, crusted side down, and cook until golden brown, 3 to 4 minutes. Flip the fish and cook until the skin is golden brown, another 2 minutes. Transfer the fish to a paper-towel-lined plate to drain. Serve hot, with the salsa.

Strawberry Daiquiris

Makes 4 servings

This cocktail is tasty with or without the alcohol. To make a virgin daiquiri, simply omit the rum and add a little water or orange juice if the mixture seems too thick.

1. Combine all the ingredients in a blender, and blend until smooth and creamy.

2. Pour the daiquiris into cocktail glasses and serve immediately.

2 cups sweetened frozen strawberries

1 cup crushed ice

1/2 cup freshly squeezed lime juice

4 ounces light rum

4 ounces dark rum

Note: Blue Cornmeal Like the white and yellow varieties, blue cornmeal is made from dried corn kernels that have been ground to a fine, medium, or coarse grind. Blue cornmeal is not as common as the other varieties, but can be purchased at specialty food stores and online at www.gourmetsleuth.com. If you cannot find blue cornmeal, yellow cornmeal will work, though the flavor will be a little sweeter and less intense.

Sesame-Crusted Mahi-Mahi

4 (8-ounce) mahi-mahi fillets

2 teaspoons toasted (Asian) sesame oil

Kosher salt and freshly ground black pepper

1/2 cup black sesame seeds, toasted (see note)

1/2 cup white sesame seeds, toasted (see note)

1 tablespoon canola oil

1 tablespoon unsalted butter

Lime wedges

I love fish, but it's not Tony's favorite. So in order for me to get Tony to enjoy it, I have to do something to make it appealing and special. The sesame gives the mahi-mahi a great crust, which Tony, the texture guy, can really appreciate. Plus the combination of black and white sesame seeds is gorgeous.

Makes 4 servings

1. Brush both sides of the fish with sesame oil. Season the fish generously on both sides with salt and pepper. In a small bowl, mix together the sesame seeds. Coat each fillet with sesame seeds, pressing on them to adhere to the fish.

2. Heat a large nonstick skillet over medium-high heat. Add the oil and butter and swirl in the pan to combine. Add the fillets to the pan, and cook, turning once, until the fish is opaque and cooked through to taste, about 4 minutes per side.

3. Transfer to a paper-towel-lined plate to drain. Serve with lime wedges.

Note: Toasting Sesame Seeds To toast sesame seeds, heat a small pan over medium heat. Add the seeds and toast, stirring occasionally, until they darken slightly and smell nutty, about 1 minute. Immediately pour the seeds onto a plate to cool.

Fish Tacos with Mango Salsa, page 65

Seafood Lasagna, page 73

Mom's Fried Chicken, page 101

Beef Wellington with Cabrales, page 122,
with Lobster Mashed Potatoes, page 144

Veal Saltimbocca, page 130,
with Wild Mushroom Risotto, page 79

Shrimp 'n' Grits, page 163

Black-Bottom Banana Cream Pie, page 177

Halibut with Spicy Soy Broth

I created this recipe about three years ago, when Tony and I were living in Washington. I like to cook fish and wanted to create a dish that was simple yet a little different. The combination of soy, sesame oil, and ginger gives it a nice Asian feel. This recipe serves only two (perfect for Tony and me), but you can double or triple it. I love it with my spicy Cumin Rice (page 149), but plain rice is good, too. **Makes 2 servings**

1. Heat a large nonstick skillet over medium-high heat until very hot, about 2 minutes. Season the halibut on both sides with salt and pepper. Add the oil to the pan, and heat until hot but not smoking. Add the halibut, skin side down, and cook for about 3 minutes. Turn the halibut and cook until golden around the edges but not cooked through, an additional 1 to 2 minutes. Transfer the halibut to a warm plate and tent with foil.

2. Reduce the heat to medium. Add the ginger, garlic, and serrano pepper. Cook until fragrant, about 30 seconds. Add the shiitakes, soy sauce, fish sauce, vinegar, sesame oil, honey, and 1/2 cup water, and bring to a boil.

3. Return the halibut to the pan, cover, and reduce the heat to medium-low. Cook until the fish is done to taste, 2 to 3 minutes more. Garnish with scallions, cilantro, and lime wedges and serve.

2 (6-ounce) halibut fillets

Kosher salt and freshly ground black pepper

1/2 tablespoon canola oil

1 tablespoon minced ginger

1 teaspoon minced garlic

1 serrano chile pepper, seeded and minced

1/2 cup sliced shiitake mushrooms

1 tablespoon low-sodium soy sauce

1 tablespoon Thai or Vietnamese fish sauce (see note, page 37)

2 teaspoons rice wine vinegar

1 teaspoon toasted (Asian) sesame oil

1 teaspoon honey

1/4 cup chopped scallions

1 tablespoon chopped fresh cilantro

2 lime wedges

Whole Trout en Papillote
with Lemon-Shallot Butter

For the lemon-shallot butter:

3 tablespoons unsalted butter, softened

1 tablespoon minced shallot

1 teaspoon freshly squeezed lemon juice

1 teaspoon finely grated lemon zest

1/4 teaspoon kosher salt

1/8 teaspoon freshly ground black pepper

2 (8- to 10-ounce) whole bone-in trout, cleaned

Kosher salt and freshly ground black pepper

1/2 cup sliced yellow onion

3/4 cup fresh herbs (such as thyme, parsley, and rosemary)

1 lemon, sliced

2 tablespoons dry white wine

1 tablespoon extra virgin olive oil

Steaming en papillote (wrapped in parchment paper) is a terrific way to prepare fish, since it cooks it gently and slowly, keeping the flesh moist, and infuses it with whatever flavors you add to the pouch. Here, I use a zesty lemon-shallot butter and plenty of fresh herbs. Since you can assemble the whole thing a couple of hours ahead, it's particularly convenient for a dinner party, so feel free to double or triple the recipe. **Makes 2 servings**

1. Preheat the oven to 400° F. Cut two sheets of parchment paper large enough to completely cover each fish when folded over.

2. To make the shallot butter, in a small bowl, mash together all the ingredients until well-combined. Chill until ready to use, or form into a log, wrap in plastic, and freeze for up to 1 month.

3. Using a very sharp knife, score the fish on one side by cutting slits into the flesh down to the bone. Season the trout generously, inside and out, with salt and pepper.

4. Spread ¼ cup onion on each sheet of parchment. Place the seasoned fish on top, scored side up. Stuff the inside of each fish with the herbs. (It's okay if the herbs stick out.) Top each fish with half of the shallot butter.

5. Arrange the lemon slices on top of each fish. Drizzle 1 tablespoon of white wine and ½ tablespoon of olive oil over each fish.

6. Fold the parchment over one fish lengthwise, with the open end of the paper facing you. Begin folding the parchment at the lower left corner, and continue to fold over the edges until you have reached

the right corner of the parchment, making sure to completely seal the folds as you go. Tuck the final fold of paper underneath itself to secure. Repeat with the remaining fish.

7. Place the fish on a large baking sheet and bake for about 15 minutes, depending on the size of the fish. To serve, transfer the trout, still in the parchment, to a platter. Cut open the parchment at the table and serve.

Blackened Catfish

Catfish is plentiful and inexpensive, and we ate a lot of it when I was growing up. It was the go-to fish for my mother. These days I cook all kinds of fish at home, but I still love catfish, especially when it's blackened in a crust of spices. Tony will happily eat anything fiery and crisp, so this is a good way to get him to eat fish. Serve it with Quick Red Beans and Rice (see page 150) for a hearty accompaniment.

Leftover spice rub can be stored, airtight, at room temperature for up to three months. You can also try it on other fish, chicken, and even pork. **Makes 6 servings**

1. To make the spice mixture, combine the paprika, garlic powder, salt, mustard, thyme, black pepper, cayenne, oregano, and sugar in a small bowl. Generously season the catfish fillets on both sides with some of the spice mixture.

2. Heat a large cast-iron skillet over medium-high heat until very hot, 3 to 5 minutes. Add 2 teaspoons of the oil and 3 of the fillets to the skillet. Cook until a knife inserted in the center goes in easily, 3 to 4 minutes on each side. Repeat with the remaining oil and fillets. Transfer to a paper-towel-lined plate, blot any excess oil, and serve immediately.

For the blackened spice mixture:

2 tablespoons paprika

2 tablespoons garlic powder

1 1/2 tablespoons kosher salt

1 tablespoon dry mustard

1 tablespoon dried thyme

1/2 tablespoon freshly ground black pepper

1/2 tablespoon cayenne pepper

1/2 tablespoon dried oregano

1 teaspoon sugar

6 (8-ounce) catfish fillets

4 teaspoons canola oil

Asian Salmon
with Ginger and Soy

4 (6- to 8-ounce) salmon
   fillets, skin removed

For the ginger-soy sauce:

1/4 cup low-sodium soy sauce

1/4 cup minced ginger

2 tablespoons rice wine
   vinegar

2 tablespoons sugar

4 teaspoons toasted (Asian)
   sesame oil

2 teaspoons minced garlic

2 teaspoons dry mustard

Kosher salt and freshly
   ground black pepper

2 tablespoons canola oil

1/4 cup chopped scallions,
   green part only

This low-calorie recipe has tons of flavor. Ginger and soy sauce are naturals with salmon because their sharp flavors cut the richness of the fish, and the sesame oil adds a nice nutty undertone. The classic side dish would be white rice, but soba noodles, my favorite, are also terrific. The Crantini is a nice, fruity beverage to serve here—not just because the pink color goes so well with the salmon, but because the fruity sweetness helps to mellow the saltiness of the soy. **Makes 4 servings**

1. Arrange the salmon in a shallow baking dish.

2. To make the ginger-soy sauce, in a small bowl, combine the soy sauce, ginger, vinegar, sugar, sesame oil, garlic, and dry mustard, and stir well. Pour the marinade over the salmon, cover tightly with plastic wrap, and refrigerate for 20 minutes.

3. Remove the salmon from the marinade. In a small saucepan over medium heat, bring the marinade and 1/4 cup water to a boil and reduce the heat to low.

4. Lightly season the salmon with salt and pepper. Heat a nonstick skillet over medium-high heat. When hot but not smoking, add the oil. Cook the salmon, turning once, until just cooked through, 3 to 5 minutes per side. Drizzle the sauce over the salmon and serve, garnished with the scallions.

Crantini (a.k.a. Cosmo)

Makes 2 servings

1. Fill a shaker halfway with ice. Add the cranberry juice, vodka, orange liqueur, grenadine, and lime juice. Cover and shake very well.

2. Strain into chilled martini glasses and serve immediately. Garnish each with a lime twist.

5 ounces cranberry juice cocktail

3 ounces premium vodka

3 ounces orange liqueur

1/2 ounce grenadine

Freshly squeezed juice of 1/2 lime

Lime twists

Baked Rockfish with Crab Imperial

I came up with this recipe when Tony and I were living in Baltimore, where the rockfish is king, and Old Bay seasoning is used on practically everything except ice cream. The crab makes this dish super luxe. When I want to save a few calories, I use Miracle Whip light, but regular mayonnaise is good, too.

Makes 4 servings

1. Preheat the oven to 375° F. Season both sides of the fish with salt and pepper, and transfer to a baking sheet covered with parchment paper or foil.

2. In a medium bowl, combine the crabmeat, bell peppers, shallot, Miracle Whip, parsley, mustard, Worcestershire sauce, garlic, Old Bay, and cayenne. Using your hands, gently mix to incorporate.

3. Place a quarter of the crab mixture on top of each fish fillet, packing down to secure it. Top each with cracker crumbs and some of the butter pieces. Bake about 25 minutes, until golden brown.

4 (4- to 6-ounce) rockfish fillets

Kosher salt and freshly ground black pepper

1 pound lump crabmeat, picked clean (see note, page 19)

1/4 cup finely diced red bell pepper

1/4 cup finely diced green bell pepper

1 small shallot, minced

3 tablespoons Miracle Whip light or mayonnaise

2 tablespoons chopped fresh flat-leaf parsley

1 tablespoon Dijon mustard

1 teaspoon Worcestershire sauce

1 teaspoon minced garlic

1 teaspoon Old Bay seasoning

1/4 teaspoon cayenne pepper

1/4 cup saltine cracker crumbs or cracker meal

2 tablespoons unsalted butter, cut into pieces

# Shrimp Creole

1 1/2 tablespoons unsalted butter

1 1/2 tablespoons canola oil

1 cup chopped onions

1/2 cup chopped green bell pepper

1/2 cup chopped red bell pepper

1/2 cup chopped celery

1 tablespoon minced garlic

2 teaspoons dried thyme

1 teaspoon kosher salt

1 teaspoon sugar, optional

3/4 teaspoon cayenne pepper

2 bay leaves

2 (28-ounce) cans crushed tomatoes

1 tablespoon Worcestershire sauce

2 teaspoons hot sauce

2 1/2 pounds medium shrimp, peeled and deveined (see note, page 20)

1 teaspoon Cajun seasoning (see note, page 54)

1/2 cup chopped scallions

2 tablespoons chopped fresh flat-leaf parsley

This is a quick dish that's perfect for a busy weekday, yet seems special because of the shrimp. Serve it over rice or with crusty bread and a salad. **Makes 8 servings**

1. In a Dutch oven over medium heat, melt the butter and oil. Add the onions, bell peppers, and celery. Cook, stirring occasionally, until the vegetables are soft, 12 to 15 minutes. Add the garlic, thyme, salt, sugar (if using), cayenne, and bay leaves.

2. Raise the heat to medium-high and add the tomatoes, Worcestershire sauce, and hot sauce. Bring the sauce to a boil and reduce the heat to medium-low. Simmer, uncovered, for 20 minutes or until the sauce has thickened. Taste and adjust the seasoning if necessary.

3. Raise the heat to medium-high. Season the shrimp with Cajun seasoning and add to the pan. Cook the shrimp until just cooked through, about 3 minutes. Discard the bay leaves. Add the scallions and parsley and serve immediately.

✳ Crawfish Étouffée

*É**touffée** means smothered, in this case with a spicy, creamy sauce flavored with thyme, onion, and bell pepper. I used to make shrimp, chicken, and crawfish étouffée regularly in Baltimore. It's an easy, quick, and very impressive dish to serve to guests. Serve this with rice. **Makes 8 servings**

1. In a large, heavy-bottomed saucepan over medium heat, melt the butter and whisk in the flour. Cook, stirring frequently, until the roux is the color of peanut butter, about 15 minutes.

2. Add the celery, bell pepper, and onion to the roux, and cook until the vegetables are soft, about 10 minutes. Add the garlic, bay leaves, and thyme, and cook for another minute. Add the stock, Worcestershire sauce, salt, and cayenne, and bring to a boil.

3. Reduce the heat to a simmer and cook, uncovered, for 20 minutes, stirring occasionally.

4. Taste and adjust the seasoning if necessary. Season the crawfish with Cajun seasoning and add to the pan, along with the lemon juice. Cook until the crawfish are heated through, about 10 minutes. Discard the bay leaves and thyme sprigs. Stir in the scallions and parsley and serve immediately.

Note: Crawfish Tails Frozen crawfish tails can be purchased at your local fish market or online at www.lacrawfish.com.

---

4 tablespoons (1/2 stick) unsalted butter

1/2 cup all-purpose flour

3/4 cup chopped celery

3/4 cup chopped green bell pepper

1/2 cup chopped onion

4 garlic cloves, minced

2 bay leaves

4 sprigs fresh thyme

4 cups fish or vegetable stock

2 teaspoons Worcestershire sauce

1 teaspoon kosher salt

1/2 teaspoon cayenne pepper

2 pounds frozen crawfish tail meat, thawed (see note)

1 teaspoon Cajun seasoning (see note, page 54)

Freshly squeezed juice of 1/2 lemon

1/2 cup chopped scallions

1/4 cup chopped fresh flat-leaf parsley

Cajun-Style King Crab Legs

2 celery stalks, roughly chopped

2 lemons, cut in half

1 large onion, roughly chopped

1 head garlic, cut in half

1 package crab boil (see note)

2 tablespoons cider vinegar

2 tablespoons kosher salt

1 tablespoon sugar

12 Alaskan king crab legs, slightly cracked

4 tablespoons (1/2 stick) melted butter, plus additional for serving

Blackened spice mixture (see Blackened Catfish, page 87)

Lemon wedges

Tony and I were regulars at a crab house in St. Louis, and that's where the inspiration for this dish came from. Tony loves these crab legs and so does the other man in my life, my brother. So this dish is a hit with both of them. I like to serve it with Gran's fruity punch. **Makes 4 servings**

1. Fill a large pot halfway with water. Add the celery, lemons, onion, garlic, crab boil, vinegar, salt, and sugar, and bring to a boil. Reduce the heat to low and simmer, uncovered, for 20 minutes. Taste and adjust the seasoning if necessary.

2. Return the liquid to a boil and add the crab legs. Simmer until the crab is cooked through and hot, about 10 minutes, depending on their size. (If the crab legs are frozen, cook for an additional minute or two.) Transfer the crab legs to a large platter. Coat with butter and sprinkle generously with the spice mixture. Serve with additional melted butter and lemon wedges.

Gran's Punch

Makes 10 servings

2 (12-ounce) cans pink-lemonade frozen concentrate

2 (12-ounce) cans strawberry-kiwi juice frozen concentrate

2 liters Sprite or other lemon-lime soda

1 cup fresh strawberries, cored and cut in half

5 kiwis, peeled and sliced

In a large punch bowl, combine all the ingredients with 10 lemonade cans full of cold water. Serve over ice.

Note: Crab Boil Crab boil is a spice mixture added to the boiling water for shrimp, crab, lobster, and fish. The blend usually includes a mixture of whole spices, like mustard seed, cloves, bay leaves, peppercorns, and caraway. Crab boil is available at many seafood markets and online at www.penzeys.com.

Deep-Fried Lobster Tails

There's a restaurant in Baltimore known for its deep-fried lobster tails, which is where I got the idea for this dish. Tony usually isn't a huge fan of lobster, but he loves pretty much anything that is deep-fried. So here I coat meaty lobster tails in a light and crunchy tempura batter, then fry them until they're golden brown. You can serve this just with lemon wedges if you don't have pink peppercorns to make the sauce. But with their sweet, almost pinelike flavor, the peppercorns really complement the succulence of the lobster. **Makes 4 servings**

For the pink peppercorn sauce:

1/4 cup sugar

2 tablespoons Champagne vinegar

2 tablespoons pink peppercorns, crushed

Peanut oil, for frying

1 1/2 cups seltzer water

2 cups self-rising cake flour

4 (6- to 8-ounce) lobster tails

Lawry's seasoned salt and freshly ground black pepper

1. To make the sauce, in a small saucepan over medium heat, combine the sugar, Champagne vinegar, and peppercorns. Simmer, stirring occasionally, until the sugar dissolves.

2. Fill a deep, heavy pot halfway with oil. Heat the pot over medium-high heat to 365° F or until a drop of flour sizzles in the oil.

3. Place the seltzer water in a large bowl and sift the flour over it. Stir to mix lightly. The batter should have lumps in it. Season the lobster with the seasoning salt and pepper. Dip each tail into the batter and gently place into the oil one at a time.

4. Cook until golden brown, 5 to 7 minutes. Transfer the tails to a paper-towel-lined plate to drain. Season immediately with additional seasoning salt. Serve with the pink peppercorn sauce for dipping.

Perfectly Poultry

Quick Chicken Piccata

3 tablespoons all-purpose flour

1 teaspoon kosher salt

1/2 teaspoon freshly ground black pepper

4 (6-ounce) skinless, boneless chicken breast halves, pounded 1/2 inch thick (see note, page 99)

2 tablespoons extra virgin olive oil

2 teaspoons minced shallot

2 teaspoons minced garlic

1/2 cup dry white wine

1 tablespoon freshly squeezed lemon juice

2/3 cup low-sodium chicken broth or stock

2 tablespoons chopped fresh flat-leaf parsley

2 tablespoons cold unsalted butter

1 tablespoon capers, rinsed and drained

1 pound linguine cooked according to package directions

This is a simple Italian dish that takes just minutes to make. Tony loves the salty tang that the capers give it and we both love how easy it is. **Makes 4 servings**

1. Place the flour, salt, and pepper in a large resealable plastic bag, and shake the bag to mix. Add the chicken and shake the bag to coat.

2. Heat the oil in a large skillet over medium-high heat. Add the chicken and cook until it's golden at the edges, about 3 minutes on each side. Transfer the chicken to a plate and tent it with foil.

3. In the same pan, sauté the shallot and garlic for about 30 seconds, until fragrant. Deglaze the pan with the wine and lemon juice, scraping up any browned bits. Cook the sauce until it's reduced by a third.

4. Add the chicken broth to the skillet and reduce the heat to medium. Cook until the sauce thickens slightly, about 5 minutes. Add the parsley, butter, and capers, stirring constantly. Taste and adjust the seasoning if necessary. Return the chicken to the pan and cook until heated through, about 2 minutes. Serve with hot linguine and crusty bread.

Chicken with Olives, Capers, and Sun-dried Tomatoes

There's always room in everyone's recipe collection for more interesting chicken dishes. Tony loves Mediterranean flavors, so I came up with this combination just for him. The sweet sun-dried tomatoes and the salty, briny green olives are a perfect match for the chicken, which I cook on the bone for extra flavor. It goes really well with couscous or rice. **Makes 6 servings**

1. Preheat the oven to 400° F.

2. Place a medium skillet over medium-high heat and warm the olive oil. Add the peppers and sauté until slightly softened, about 3 minutes. Add the garlic and sauté 1 minute more. Transfer the peppers to a medium bowl.

3. Arrange the chicken breasts in a 13 X 9-inch roasting pan and season with salt and pepper on both sides. To the bell pepper mixture, add the olives, sherry, thyme, capers, and onion powder (if using), and mix well. Cover the chicken with the mixture, and cook, uncovered, for 20 minutes. Add the sun-dried tomatoes and continue to roast until the chicken is cooked through, about 10 minutes more.

1 tablespoon extra virgin olive oil

1/2 cup sliced red bell pepper

1/2 cup sliced green bell pepper

4 garlic cloves, sliced

6 bone-in, skinless chicken breast halves

Kosher salt and freshly ground black pepper

22 green olives, preferably picholine, pitted and chopped

1/4 cup dry sherry

Leaves from 5 sprigs fresh thyme

1 tablespoon capers, rinsed

1 teaspoon onion powder, optional

1/4 cup oil-packed sun-dried tomatoes, drained and sliced lengthwise into strips

Chicken Parmesan

For the marinara sauce:

2 teaspoons extra virgin olive oil

1 cup chopped red bell pepper

1/2 cup chopped sweet onion (such as Vidalia)

3 garlic cloves, thinly sliced

1 (28-ounce) can diced tomatoes, with juice

1 teaspoon kosher salt

1 teaspoon sugar, optional

1/2 teaspoon dried oregano

1/2 teaspoon crushed red pepper flakes

3 tablespoons fresh basil, cut into a chiffonade (see note, page 32)

2 tablespoons chopped fresh flat-leaf parsley

4 (4-ounce) boneless, skinless chicken breast halves, pounded 1/4 inch thick (see note)

Kosher salt and freshly ground black pepper

1/2 cup Italian bread crumbs

1/2 cup freshly grated Parmigiano-Reggiano cheese

2 large eggs, lightly beaten

2 tablespoons whole milk

2 tablespoons extra virgin olive oil

Cooking spray

1 cup grated part-skim or whole-milk mozzarella cheese

1 pound linguine cooked according to package directions

Ah, chicken parmesan; Tony's favorite chicken dish. It gets its savory crispiness from the bread crumbs and Parmesan, and the quick marinara sauce I coat it with gives it a tangy kick. You can make the sauce a day or two ahead and reheat it just before serving. I like to pair this with a salad and crusty bread. **Makes 4 servings**

1. To prepare the sauce, in a large saucepan over medium-high heat, heat the olive oil. Add the bell pepper and onion and sauté until soft, about 10 minutes. Add the garlic and cook until it begins to brown, about 1 minute. Add the canned tomatoes with their juice, salt, sugar (if using), oregano, and crushed red pepper. Bring to a boil, cover, reduce the heat to low, and simmer for 10 minutes.

2. Taste and adjust the seasoning if necessary. Remove the sauce from the heat and add the basil and parsley.

3. Preheat the oven to 350° F. Season the chicken on both sides with salt and pepper. Combine the bread crumbs and Parmigiano-Reggiano cheese in a shallow dish. In another shallow dish, whisk the eggs with the milk. Dip each breast half in the egg wash, then dredge in the bread-crumb mixture.

4. In a large nonstick skillet over medium-high heat, warm the oil. Add the chicken and cook, in batches if necessary, until golden, about 3 minutes on each side.

5. Arrange the chicken in a 13 X 9-inch baking dish coated with cooking spray. Pour the sauce over the chicken and sprinkle evenly with the mozzarella. Bake for 15 minutes. Serve hot, over the linguine.

Note: Scaloppine The term *scaloppine* refers to meat, usually veal but sometimes chicken or turkey, that has been pounded very thin. To prepare it, place the meat in a resealable plastic bag (but keep it unsealed) or between two sheets of wax paper. Using a meat pounder, gently pound the meat until it's thin.

✳ Cornbread-Stuffed Chicken Roulade

This dish was one of my first forays into the gourmet world of creating my own recipes. Ten years ago, I came across a chicken dish filled with a vegetable-and-bread stuffing. I thought a Cajun-flavored cornbread filling would be a delicious variation, and it was. This dish presents beautifully. I love making it for guests. **Makes 4 servings**

1. Preheat the oven to 350° F.

2. Heat a medium skillet over medium heat. Add the oil, onion, celery, and bell peppers, and cook until soft, about 5 minutes. Add the garlic, Cajun seasoning, and thyme, and cook until fragrant, about 30 seconds. Transfer to a large bowl.

3. Add the cornbread, chicken broth, scallions, hot sauce, and Worcestershire sauce to the bowl. Mix until combined. Taste and adjust the seasoning if necessary.

4. Place about ¼ cup of stuffing into the center of each chicken breast. Roll lengthwise and secure with a toothpick. Transfer the chicken roulades to a large baking dish. Bake, uncovered, about 30 minutes, until the juices run clear when pricked with a fork. Do not overcook.

1 tablespoon canola oil

1/2 cup chopped onion

1/4 cup chopped celery

2 tablespoons chopped green bell pepper

2 tablespoons chopped red bell pepper

1 tablespoon minced garlic

1 1/2 teaspoons Cajun seasoning (see note, page 54)

1 teaspoon dried thyme

2 cups cubed cornbread

1/2 cup low-sodium chicken broth or stock

4 scallions, chopped

6 dashes hot sauce

4 dashes Worcestershire sauce

Kosher salt and freshly ground black pepper

4 skinless, boneless chicken breast halves, pounded 1/4 inch thick (see note above)

Levon's Coastal Curry Chicken

3 bone-in, skinless whole chicken breasts (2¹/2 to 3 pounds)

Kosher salt and freshly ground black pepper

2 tablespoons vegetable oil

2 large white onions, chopped

3 tablespoons Madras curry powder

1 tablespoon minced garlic

1 tablespoon minced ginger

1 teaspoon mild chili powder

1 teaspoon ground cumin

1 teaspoon ground cinnamon

4 cups low-sodium chicken broth or stock

1¹/2 ripe bananas, mashed (about 3/4 cup)

2 bay leaves

3 small sweet potatoes, peeled and cut into 1/2-inch cubes (about 1¹/2 pounds)

When my brother, Levon, and I lived in Miami, he got friendly with a Jamaican chef. This dish is the result of that friendship. I like to serve it with yogurt and jasmine rice, which soaks up all the good curry sauce. Sweet mango iced tea is a terrific beverage here if you don't want beer.

Makes 6 servings

1. Heat a wide Dutch oven over medium-high heat. Season the chicken well with salt and pepper. Add the oil to the pan and brown the chicken in the oil until well-browned on all sides (work in batches if necessary), about 15 minutes. Transfer the chicken to a plate.

2. Pour off all but 1 tablespoon of the fat in the pot. Add the onions and cook, stirring occasionally, until they are slightly golden, about 10 minutes. Reduce the heat to medium and add the curry, garlic, ginger, chili powder, cumin, and cinnamon. Cook, stirring constantly, until very fragrant, 2 to 3 minutes.

3. Add the broth, bananas, and bay leaves, and bring to a boil. Season with salt to taste. Add the chicken and sweet potatoes, reduce the heat, and simmer, partially covered, until the chicken is cooked through (the juices will run clear when the chicken is pierced to the bone), about 40 minutes. Transfer the chicken to a cutting board. Raise the heat to medium and simmer, uncovered, until the sauce is thickened and the sweet potatoes are thoroughly tender, 5 to 15 minutes more. Discard the bay leaves.

4. Meanwhile, cut the chicken off the bone and into bite-size pieces. When the sweet potatoes are cooked, return the chicken to the pot to warm it. Serve immediately.

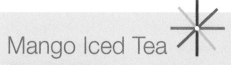

Mango Iced Tea

Makes 8 servings

1. Place the tea bags in a large heat-proof bowl or pitcher. Bring 8 cups of water to a boil. Pour the water over the tea bags. Steep the tea for 10 minutes, then remove and discard the tea bags. Cool the tea and chill, covered, until cold, about 1 hour.

2. To make simple syrup, in a medium saucepan, bring the sugar and 1/3 cup of water to a boil, stirring until the sugar is completely dissolved. Let the syrup cool, and chill, covered. (The syrup may be made up to 3 weeks ahead and stored in a covered container in the refrigerator.)

3. Place the tea, syrup, nectar, mint, and vanilla in a large pitcher and stir well. Serve the tea over ice in tall glasses and garnish with fresh mint sprigs.

6 orange pekoe tea bags

1/3 cup sugar

6 cups mango nectar, chilled

1/2 cup fresh mint leaves, plus sprigs for garnish

2 teaspoons vanilla extract

Mom's Fried Chicken

Nobody makes fried chicken better than my mom. Not even me. She's got the touch. But I have picked up some of her tricks. One is that soaking the chicken in buttermilk makes it very juicy. Another is her spice mix, which can't be beat. Tony requests this chicken every chance he gets. Serve it with homemade strawberry lemonade for the ultimate summer lunch. **Makes 8 servings**

1. In a large nonreactive bowl or other large container, combine the chicken pieces and the buttermilk. Cover and refrigerate for at least 8 hours or overnight.

8 bone-in, skinless chicken breasts, cut in half

16 chicken wings

1 quart low-fat buttermilk

Peanut oil, for frying

1 tablespoon Lawry's seasoned salt

1 tablespoon paprika

1 tablespoon garlic powder

1 tablespoon freshly ground black pepper

Kosher salt

4 cups all-purpose flour

2. Add about 3 inches of peanut oil to a fryer or large pot. Heat the oil over medium heat until very hot (365° F on a deep-frying thermometer; a pinch of flour will sizzle immediately when dropped into the oil), about 4 minutes. Line a rimmed baking sheet with paper towels and set a wire rack on top.

3. Combine the seasoned salt, paprika, garlic powder, and black pepper. Season the chicken generously on both sides with kosher salt and the seasoning mix. Place the flour in a large resealable plastic bag and add a few pieces of chicken at a time. Shake the bag to coat the chicken. Remove the pieces from the bag and shake off the excess flour. Do this step right before the oil is ready.

4. Preheat the oven to 225° F. Place the chicken in the hot oil. Do not crowd the pan. Fry the chicken in batches until golden, about 10 minutes per side. Transfer the chicken to the wire rack over the baking sheet to drain, and place the baking sheet in the oven to keep warm. Repeat with the remaining chicken.

Strawberry Lemonade

Makes about 1 1/2 quarts

1 cup sugar

Freshly squeezed juice and peeled zest of 8 lemons

2 cups frozen strawberries, pureed

8 lemon slices

1. In a small saucepan, bring 1 cup of water, the sugar, and the lemon zest to a boil. Cook until the sugar is dissolved and let cool.

2. Pass the strawberry puree through a sieve into a large pitcher. Add 5 cups of water, the lemon juice, and the sugar syrup. Stir well and chill, covered, until very cold. The lemonade will keep for 2 days, refrigerated. Serve garnished with the lemon slices.

Seared Duck Breasts
with Cherry Port Sauce

Duck with fruit is a classic no-brainer. But Tony isn't a fan of the dish if it's very sweet and cloying. Cherries have a nice sweetness, but they are not overpowering. And the combination of port, vinegar, and veal stock definitely takes the sauce to the savory side. If you can't find Muscovy duck breasts, you can use duck magret, though you'll need only three instead of four, since they are bigger. Serve this with regular or wild rice. **Makes 4 servings**

1. Place a small saucepan over medium heat and warm the oil. Add the shallot and cook until soft, about 2 minutes. Add the cherries, orange juice, stock, port, lime juice, vinegar, and honey (if using). Bring to a boil and reduce the heat to low. Cook until the sauce is reduced by half and has thickened significantly, about 25 minutes. Taste and adjust the seasoning if necessary.

2. Heat a large, heavy-bottomed skillet over medium heat. Season the duck generously on both sides with salt and pepper. Place the duck breasts in the pan, skin side down. Sear the duck until it's brown and crispy and the fat has rendered, 10 to 12 minutes. Turn the duck over and cook the meat until it's cooked through, about 3 minutes more. Transfer the duck to a cutting board and allow it to rest for 3 to 5 minutes, then cut it diagonally against the grain, keeping each breast in one piece.

3. To serve, place the sauce in the center of a plate. Place the duck, skin side up, on top of the sauce, fanning it out to display the juicy meat and crisp skin.

1 teaspoon extra virgin olive oil

1/2 cup chopped shallot

12 frozen dark sweet cherries

1 cup freshly squeezed orange juice

1 cup veal stock or low-sodium beef broth or stock

1/2 cup tawny port

1/4 cup freshly squeezed lime juice

2 tablespoons balsamic vinegar

1 teaspoon honey, optional

Kosher salt and freshly ground black pepper

4 (8-ounce) boneless Muscovy duck breast halves, scored and trimmed

Herb-Roasted Turkey

12 tablespoons (1 1/2 sticks) unsalted butter, softened

1/4 cup packed fresh flat-leaf parsley leaves, chopped, plus 4 whole sprigs

1 large sprig fresh rosemary, leaves chopped, plus 2 whole sprigs

1 tablespoon chopped fresh thyme, plus 4 whole sprigs

15 leaves fresh sage, chopped, plus 3 whole leaves

3/4 teaspoon kosher salt, plus more for the turkey

1/2 teaspoon freshly ground black pepper, plus more for the turkey

1 (15-pound) turkey

1 lemon, quartered

8 shallots, peeled and halved

1 head garlic, cloves separated and peeled

4 cups low-sodium chicken broth or stock

2/3 cup dry white wine

3 tablespoons all-purpose flour

Thanksgiving dinner was a big deal when I was growing up, and I was helping my grandmother with the cooking by the time I was not much taller than the counter. I specialized in the side dishes—the macaroni and cheese, yams, and greens—and the pies, and left the turkey and dressing up to my grandmother. The first time I ever made this herb-roasted turkey, I was twenty-one and cooking a small Thanksgiving meal for just Tony and me. Tony was playing for the Rams at the time and we couldn't get home for the holiday. So I came up with this recipe and now it's my Thanksgiving standard. Regular roast turkey can be bland, but not mine. The herb butter gives such amazing flavor and adds moisture, so the turkey doesn't dry out. **Makes 10 servings**

1. In a small bowl, combine the butter, chopped parsley, chopped rosemary, chopped thyme, chopped sage, salt, and pepper, and mix well.

2. Position a rack in the bottom third of the oven and preheat the oven to 450° F. Sprinkle the main cavity of the turkey with salt and pepper. Place the whole sprigs of parsley, rosemary, and thyme and the sage leaves into the cavity. Add the lemon, 4 shallot halves, and half of the garlic cloves.

3. Starting at the neck end, carefully slide a hand between the skin and the breast meat to loosen the skin. Spread 3 tablespoons of the herb butter over the breast meat under the skin. Tuck the wing tips under the skin, and tie the legs together to hold the shape. Season the turkey generously all over with salt and pepper.

4. Place the turkey on a wire rack set in a large roasting pan. Rub 4 tablespoons of the herb butter over the turkey. Roast about 30 minutes, until golden brown, and reduce the heat to 350° F. Baste the turkey with ½ cup of broth. Cover only the breast area with a sheet of heavy-duty aluminum foil. Scatter the remaining shallots and garlic cloves in the pan around the turkey.

5. Continue roasting the turkey for about 1½ hours, basting with ½ cup of broth every 30 minutes. Remove the foil from the turkey breast. Continue to roast the turkey, basting with pan juices every 20 minutes, about 1 hour longer, until it's golden brown and a thermometer inserted into the thickest part of the thigh registers 165° F. Transfer the turkey to a platter and brush with 1 tablespoon of the herb butter. Tent it loosely with foil and let it rest for 20 minutes before carving.

6. Using a slotted spoon, transfer the shallots and garlic from the roasting pan to a plate. Transfer the pan juices to a medium bowl, then skim off and discard the fat. Set the pan over two burners on medium-high heat. Deglaze the pan with the wine and 1 cup of chicken broth, scraping up any browned bits. Bring the sauce to a boil, reduce the heat to medium, and cook until it's reduced by half, about 4 minutes. Pour the sauce into a large measuring glass. Add the degreased pan juices, and broth, if necessary, to equal 3 cups liquid.

7. Blend the flour into the remaining herb butter until combined. Pour the broth mixture into a medium saucepan and bring to a boil. Gradually whisk in the herb-butter mixture. Add any accumulated juices from the turkey platter and boil until the gravy thickens enough to coat a spoon, whisking occasionally, about 6 minutes. Add the shallots and garlic to the gravy and simmer for 1 minute. Taste and adjust the seasoning if necessary. Serve the turkey with the gravy.

Ultimate Chile Relleno
with Three Sauces

2 tablespoons coriander seeds

2 tablespoons cumin seeds

1 tablespoon whole black peppercorns

Cooking spray

6 skinless, boneless chicken breast halves

For the black bean and corn relish:

2 ears fresh sweet corn, shucked

1 tablespoon extra virgin olive oil, plus additional

1 (15.5-ounce) can black beans, rinsed and drained

2 medium tomatoes, seeded and chopped

1/2 medium red onion, finely chopped

1 jalapeño pepper, seeded and minced

1/4 cup chopped fresh cilantro

1 to 2 teaspoons honey, to taste

Freshly squeezed juice of 1 lime

1 teaspoon minced garlic

Kosher salt and freshly ground black pepper

For the roasted chile sauce:

4 large tomatoes, quartered

2 jalapeño peppers, cut in half and seeded

1 medium onion, roughly chopped

4 garlic cloves, peeled

1 tablespoon extra virgin olive oil

Tony and I used to go to an amazing authentic Mexican restaurant in San Diego, and they made a chile relleno to die for. This is my version, except it's not deep-fried, like it usually is. This is a very involved recipe, so make it on the weekend when you have extra time. It's worth every minute. Or, as a shortcut, serve it with just one of the sauces.

Makes 6 servings

1. In a dry sauté pan over low heat, toast the coriander, cumin, and black peppercorns until fragrant, about 1 minute. Transfer the spices to a spice grinder and finely grind.

2. Preheat the broiler and coat a broiler pan with cooking spray. Arrange the chicken on the pan and spray with more cooking spray. Broil the chicken in the upper third of the oven until the juices run clear, about 4 minutes per side. Transfer the chicken to a plate to cool. Once cooled, chop the chicken into small pieces and transfer to a large bowl. Stir in the ground spices. Cover with aluminum foil.

3. To make the black bean and corn relish, preheat the oven to 450° F. Rub each ear of corn lightly with olive oil, and roast in the oven until the kernels blister, about 20 minutes. Set the corn aside to cool until it is cool enough to handle, then, using a sharp knife, cut the kernels from the cob.

4. In a medium bowl, combine the black beans, corn, tomatoes, red onion, jalapeño, cilantro, honey, lime juice, 1 tablespoon of olive oil, garlic, and salt and pepper, and mix well. Cover and refrigerate for at least 1 hour.

5. To make the roasted chile sauce, preheat the broiler. In a bowl, toss together the tomatoes, jalapeños, onion, and garlic with the olive oil. On a large baking sheet, spread the tomato mixture in a single layer and broil 6 to 8 minutes, until charred. Remove from the oven and let cool, then transfer to a blender and puree until smooth.

6. Heat a medium saucepan over medium heat. Add the canola oil and whisk in the flour to combine. Cook, stirring constantly, until the roux is the color of peanut butter, about 15 minutes. Whisk in the chicken broth, charred-tomato puree, and chile powder, and bring to a boil. Reduce the heat to medium and cook, uncovered, until the flavors meld, about 15 minutes. Taste and adjust the seasoning if necessary.

7. To make the poblano filling, heat a small saucepan over medium-high heat. Add the oil, bell peppers, and onion, and cook until slightly soft, 3 to 5 minutes. Transfer the peppers and onion to the bowl with the reserved chicken. Add both cheeses, the cilantro, and 1 cup of the chile sauce, and mix well. Taste and adjust the seasoning if necessary.

8. Preheat the oven to 375° F. Using a clean towel, remove the charred skin from the poblanos. Cut a slit from stem to end, making sure not to go through the pepper. Use a spoon to remove the seeds. Stuff the peppers with the chicken mixture (about ½ cup per pepper) and secure with a toothpick. Arrange the peppers in a single layer in a large baking dish. (This recipe can be made 1 day in advance up to this point. Cover with foil and refrigerate. Bring to room temperature 30 minutes prior to cooking.) Cover with the remaining chile sauce, and bake, uncovered, until the cheese has melted and the sauce is bubbly, 20 to 30 minutes.

9. While the peppers are cooking, make the avocado salsa. In a medium bowl, combine the avocados, onion, cilantro, honey (if using), lime juice, salt and pepper to taste, and mix well. Serve the peppers hot, topped with the salsa and the black bean and corn relish.

1/4 cup canola oil

1/2 cup all-purpose flour

4 cups low-sodium chicken broth or stock

2 tablespoons ancho chile powder (see note, page 35)

Kosher salt and freshly ground black pepper

For the poblano filling:

1 tablespoon extra virgin olive oil

1/2 cup chopped red bell pepper

1/2 cup chopped orange bell pepper

1/2 cup chopped onion

1/2 cup grated Monterey Jack cheese

1/2 cup grated sharp Cheddar cheese

1/2 cup chopped fresh cilantro

6 large roasted, but not peeled, poblano peppers, stems on (see box, page 51)

For the avocado salsa:

3 ripe avocados, chopped

1/2 cup finely chopped onion

1/4 cup chopped fresh cilantro

1 teaspoon honey, optional

Freshly squeezed juice of 1 lime

1 teaspoon kosher salt, or more

Freshly ground black pepper

Mom's Stuffed Cabbage

1 large head of cabbage

2 tablespoons extra virgin olive oil

1 pound ground turkey (should be a combination of white and dark meat) or ground beef

1 teaspoon kosher salt, plus more for seasoning the meat

3/4 teaspoon freshly ground black pepper, plus more for seasoning the meat

1 cup cooked rice, cooled

1/2 green bell pepper, finely chopped

1/2 medium onion, finely chopped

2 garlic cloves, minced

1 (28-ounce) can crushed tomatoes

1/4 cup freshly grated Parmigiano-Reggiano cheese

1 teaspoon dried oregano

1 teaspoon dried basil

1/2 teaspoon dried thyme

1/4 teaspoon sugar

This is one of my mom's signature dishes, and she made it often when I was growing up. The leftover stuffing is delicious when baked by itself, like a little meat loaf. Just transfer it to a small ovenproof dish and bake it alongside the rolls. **Makes 6 servings**

1. Preheat the oven to 350° F. Bring a large pot of salted water to a boil. Plunge the head of cabbage in the water for 1 minute, remove, then peel off the softened leaves. Repeat until you have removed 12 large leaves. Return the loose leaves to the boiling water and blanch until slightly softened, 2 minutes more. Drain on a paper-towel-lined plate.

2. Place a medium nonstick skillet over medium-high heat, and add the olive oil. Add the turkey, season with salt and pepper, and cook until browned, about 10 minutes.

3. In a large bowl, combine the turkey, rice, bell pepper, onion, and garlic.

4. In a small bowl, combine the tomatoes, cheese, oregano, basil, salt, pepper, thyme, and sugar, and mix well. Add 1/3 of the tomato mixture to the turkey mixture and mix well.

5. Place 2 heaping tablespoons of the meat mixture in the center of a cabbage leaf and roll up like a burrito. Place the cabbage rolls in a baking dish. Repeat until you have made 12 rolls.

6. Cover the rolls with the remaining tomato sauce. Bake, covered, for 40 minutes.

Best-Ever Beef

Garlic Pot Roast

4 pounds boneless chuck blade pot roast, tied with butcher twine

10 garlic cloves, cut lengthwise into thirds

1 teaspoon kosher salt

3/4 teaspoon freshly ground black pepper

2 tablespoons canola oil

1 cup finely chopped onions

1/2 cup finely chopped celery

1/2 cup finely chopped green bell pepper

6 sprigs fresh thyme

2 bay leaves

4 cups beef stock, or more as needed

4 tablespoons (1/2 stick) unsalted butter, melted

4 tablespoons all-purpose flour

Tony's mom makes the best pot roast ever! She taught me her secret ten years ago; the trick is to make slits in the beef and insert slivers of garlic so it gets flavored throughout. Tony's crazy about garlic, especially when the flavor becomes sweet and mellow inside the roast. Who wouldn't be? Serve this dish with gravy and mashed potatoes. **Makes 6 to 8 servings**

1. Preheat the oven to 350° F. Using the tip of a sharp paring knife, make small slits all over roast. Insert the garlic pieces deep inside the slits. Season the roast generously with salt and pepper all over.

2. In a Dutch oven over medium-high heat, warm the oil until hot but not smoking. Sear the roast until brown on all sides, 15 to 20 minutes total. Transfer the roast to a plate with the pan juices.

3. Reduce the heat to medium. Add the onions, celery, and green pepper to the pan, and cook, stirring, until soft, about 5 minutes. Return the roast to the pan, along with the thyme, bay leaves, and enough stock to come halfway up the roast.

4. Bring the liquid to a boil, then cover the pot tightly and place it in the lower third of the oven. Cook, turning the meat several times, until the beef is fork-tender, 2½ to 3 hours.

5. Transfer the meat to a cutting board, tent it with foil to keep it warm, and let it stand 10 minutes. Skim off any fat from the surface of the pan juices, then strain and measure the liquid.

6. For the gravy, return the pan juices to the pot and bring to a boil. For each cup of liquid, stir together 1 tablespoon of butter and 1 tablespoon of flour in a small bowl. Whisk this butter-flour roux into the broth. Simmer, stirring constantly, until the gravy reaches the desired thickness. Skim off any fat that rises to the top, slice the pot roast, and serve with the gravy.

Personal Three-Meat Meat Loaves

Three different types of meat in one dish makes Tony a very happy camper. And I love individual/personal servings. These are so cute, and your guests will feel special having their own portions. Kids will love these, too. **Makes 8 servings**

1. In a 10-inch skillet over medium heat, melt the butter. Add the green pepper, onion, and celery, and cook, stirring occasionally, until soft, 3 to 5 minutes. Add the garlic and cook, stirring, for 30 seconds. Transfer the vegetables to a large bowl and let cool.

2. Once the vegetables have completely cooled, add the meat, bread crumbs, ketchup, tomato sauce, egg, Worcestershire sauce, cheese, parsley, tomato paste, salt, basil, oregano, and black pepper. Using your hands, mix thoroughly.

3. Shape the meat mixture into 8 individual loaves. Place them on a parchment-lined baking sheet, cover with plastic wrap, and refrigerate for at least 1 hour or overnight.

4. Preheat the oven to 450° F. Bake for 15 minutes, then reduce the heat to 350° F and bake 35 to 45 minutes more, until cooked through.

1 1/2 tablespoons unsalted butter

1 cup chopped green bell pepper

1 large onion, chopped

1 celery stalk, sliced

2 garlic cloves, minced

2 pounds meat loaf mix (beef, pork, and veal)

1/2 cup fine dry bread crumbs

1/3 cup ketchup

1/4 cup tomato sauce

1 egg, beaten

2 tablespoons Worcestershire sauce

2 tablespoons grated Parmigiano-Reggiano cheese

2 tablespoons chopped fresh flat-leaf parsley

1 tablespoon tomato paste

2 teaspoons kosher salt

1 teaspoon dried basil, crushed

1 teaspoon dried oregano, crushed

1 teaspoon freshly ground black pepper

Homey Braised Short Ribs

6 pounds beef short ribs, excess fat removed, rinsed and dried

Kosher salt and freshly ground black pepper

All-purpose flour

2 tablespoons extra virgin olive oil

2 carrots, chopped

2 celery stalks, chopped

1 medium onion, chopped

1 tablespoon minced garlic

10 sprigs fresh thyme

3 bay leaves

1/2 bottle dry red wine

3 cups low-sodium chicken broth or stock

1 (14-ounce) can diced tomatoes

1 (6-ounce) can tomato paste

4 scallions, chopped

1/4 cup chopped fresh flat-leaf parsley

1 pound egg noodles, cooked al dente

perfected this dish when we were living in Washington, D.C., where the winters can be so cold you'd need a really compelling reason to go outside. But there'd be nothing better to come home to than this soul-warming dish. The key is to cook the meat until it's so tender that you need only a spoon to eat it. This tastes best if you make it a day ahead. Chill it overnight, skim off any fat that's come up to the surface, and reheat it before serving. **Makes 6 servings**

1. Season the short ribs generously with salt and pepper. Sprinkle flour over the ribs to coat lightly, and shake off excess flour. Heat a Dutch oven over medium-high heat until hot, about 3 minutes.

2. Add the oil and brown the short ribs in batches, making sure not to overcrowd the pan, about 8 minutes per batch. Transfer the ribs to a plate, and set aside.

3. Reduce the heat to medium. Add the carrots, celery, and onion, and sauté until soft, 6 to 8 minutes. Add the garlic, thyme, and bay leaves, and cook until fragrant, about 30 seconds. Add the wine, broth, tomatoes, tomato paste, browned ribs, and accumulated juices from the plate.

4. Bring to a boil, cover partially, and reduce the heat to low. Cook, stirring occasionally, until the meat is very tender and falling off the bone, about 3 hours. Using a slotted spoon, transfer the meat to a bowl.

5. If necessary, reduce the braising liquid so that it resembles a sauce rather than a broth. Taste and adjust the seasoning if necessary. Discard the bay leaves and thyme sprigs. Return the ribs to the pot and heat through. Add the scallions and parsley, and serve hot over egg noodles.

Gran's Beef Stroganoff

As you already know, Tony is a big beef guy. He especially loves a beef dish served with egg noodles. My gran and my mom used to make this dish when I was growing up, and it instantly became one of Tony's most requested dinners. It's incredibly flavorful and the meat is so tender, it just melts in your mouth. **Makes 8 servings**

1. Heat a Dutch oven over medium-high heat and place some flour in a shallow bowl. Season the brisket cubes generously with salt and pepper, then dredge them in the flour. Pour 1½ tablespoons of olive oil into the pan and heat briefly. Shake the excess flour from the brisket and sear the beef in the pan until very brown all over, 10 to 12 minutes.

2. Transfer the beef to a paper-towel-lined plate and set aside. Reduce the heat to medium, and add the onions. Cook, stirring, until the onions begin to brown, 6 to 8 minutes. Add the mushrooms and cook, stirring, until they are slightly soft, 3 to 5 minutes.

3. Add the garlic, thyme leaves, and bay leaves, and cook and stir for 30 seconds more. Transfer the vegetables to a bowl.

4. Pour the remaining ¼ cup of oil into the pan, let it warm for a few seconds, then add the ¼ cup of flour, whisking until the mixture turns pale golden, about 3 minutes. Raise the heat to medium-high, pour in the wine, and bring to a boil, stirring and scraping up the browned bits from the bottom of the pan. Simmer until the liquid is reduced by a third. Pour in the beef stock, ¾ teaspoon of salt, ¾ teaspoon of pepper, the Worcestershire sauce, beef, and mushroom mixture, and bring to a simmer. Reduce the heat to low, cover partially, and simmer, stirring occasionally, until the beef is fork-tender and the sauce coats the back of a spoon, 1½ to 2 hours.

1/4 cup all-purpose flour, plus additional for dredging

11/4 pounds beef brisket, cut into 1-inch cubes

3/4 teaspoon kosher salt, plus additional for seasoning the meat

3/4 teaspoon freshly ground black pepper, plus additional for seasoning the meat

1/4 cup plus 11/2 tablespoons extra virgin olive oil

11/2 cups sliced yellow onions

2 cups sliced cremini mushrooms

1 tablespoon minced garlic

Leaves from 5 sprigs fresh thyme

2 bay leaves

1/2 cup red wine

31/2 cups beef stock

1 tablespoon Worcestershire sauce

1/2 cup low-fat sour cream

2 tablespoons chopped fresh flat-leaf parsley

1 pound egg noodles, cooked al dente

Crusty garlic bread

5. Taste and adjust the seasoning if necessary. Add the sour cream, stirring constantly, and cook for 2 minutes more. Just before serving, add the parsley.

6. Place the hot noodles in a large serving bowl. Add a third of the sauce to the noodles and stir to combine. Spoon the beef mixture on top and serve family-style, with crusty garlic bread.

Note: You can make this dish a day in advance. (Don't add the sour cream until the day you serve it.) Cool it completely before refrigerating. Warm the dish over medium-low heat for 15 minutes, add the sour cream, and cook for 5 minutes more.

✳ Osso Buco with Gremolata

3 pounds veal shanks, cut into 1 1/2-inch pieces

Kosher salt and freshly ground black pepper

All-purpose flour, for dredging

1/4 cup extra virgin olive oil

1 cup chopped onions

1/3 cup chopped carrot

1/3 cup chopped celery

3 garlic cloves, minced

3 cups low-sodium chicken broth or stock

1 cup dry white wine

1 cup fresh or canned diced tomatoes, with juice

1 tablespoon sugar, optional

4 sprigs fresh thyme

2 bay leaves

When we lived in Baltimore, we dined in Little Italy on a regular basis. One of our favorite restaurants specialized in osso buco, and it quickly became the go-to dish for Tony. In fact, Tony didn't even have to order it; as soon as we walked in the door, they started to prepare it. And they were never wrong. **Makes 4 to 6 servings**

1. Season the veal pieces generously with salt and pepper and dredge them in flour. In a Dutch oven over medium-high heat, warm the oil. Working in batches, sear the veal until very brown on all sides, 6 to 8 minutes. Transfer the meat to a plate.

2. Reduce the heat to medium. Add the onions, carrot, and celery, and cook, stirring, until soft, 5 to 7 minutes. Add the garlic, and cook and stir for 30 seconds. Pour in the broth, wine, tomatoes with juice, sugar (if using), thyme, and bay leaves.

3. Return the shanks to the pot, and bring the liquid to a boil. Cover and reduce the heat to low. Simmer until the meat is almost falling off the bone, about 1½ hours. Use a slotted spoon to transfer the meat to a bowl.

4. Bring the sauce to a boil over medium-high heat. Simmer until it has reduced to the desired consistency, 15 to 20 minutes. Taste and adjust the seasoning if necessary. Return the veal to the pot, and reduce the heat to low. Cook until the shanks are heated through, about 10 minutes more. Discard the bay leaves and thyme sprigs.

5. In a small bowl, stir together the ingredients for the gremolata. Serve the veal family-style over polenta, with the gremolata on the side.

For the gremolata:

2 tablespoons finely chopped fresh flat-leaf parsley

1 tablespoon extra virgin olive oil

1 tablespoon freshly squeezed lemon juice

Finely grated zest of 1 lemon

1 teaspoon honey, or to taste

2 garlic cloves, minced

Kosher salt and freshly ground black pepper

Cooked polenta (see box below)

Basic Polenta

Makes 4 to 6 servings

If you like polenta with a creamier consistency, add more stock or water.

1. In a large saucepan over medium-high heat, bring the chicken stock, salt, and 3 cups of water to a boil. Reduce the heat to medium, and pour in the polenta in a slow, steady stream, stirring with a wooden spoon to prevent lumps. Cook, stirring constantly, until thickened, 5 to 6 minutes.

2. Take the pan off the heat and stir in the cheese, butter, and pepper. Serve immediately.

3 cups chicken stock

2 teaspoons kosher salt

1 3/4 cups instant polenta

1/2 cup freshly grated Parmigiano-Reggiano cheese

3 tablespoons unsalted butter

Freshly ground black pepper

Szechuan Beef 'n' Veggies

1 (20-ounce) sirloin steak, trimmed and thinly sliced

3 tablespoons cornstarch

1/4 cup low-sodium beef broth or stock

2 tablespoons soy sauce

2 tablespoons Thai chili paste (see note, page 23)

1 tablespoon hoisin sauce

2 teaspoons rice wine vinegar

1 teaspoon Thai or Vietnamese fish sauce (see note, page 37)

1 teaspoon toasted (Asian) sesame oil

1 tablespoon peanut oil

2 tablespoons minced ginger

1 tablespoon minced garlic

2 cups chopped bok choy

1 cup broccoli florets

1 cup sliced red bell pepper

1/2 cup sliced onion

2 carrots, thinly sliced

4 scallions, chopped

3 cups steamed white or brown rice

This is another dish Tony and I agree on. He loves the beef, I love all the veggies in it, and we both love the hot and spicy sauce. If you don't like beef, substitute chicken; it's just as yummy. **Makes 4 servings**

1. In a medium bowl, toss the beef with 1 tablespoon of the cornstarch and let sit for 30 minutes.

2. In a small bowl, whisk together the beef broth, remaining 2 tablespoons of cornstarch, soy sauce, chili paste, hoisin sauce, vinegar, fish sauce, and sesame oil until smooth.

3. Before you begin cooking, prepare and assemble all the ingredients. Heat a wok or large nonstick skillet over high heat for 1 minute. Reduce the heat to medium-high and add the peanut oil. Add the beef and cook, stirring, for 2 minutes. Transfer the beef to a plate.

4. Add the ginger and garlic to the wok, and cook, stirring, for 30 seconds. Add the bok choy, broccoli, bell pepper, onion, and carrots, and cook, stirring often, until softened, about 3 minutes. Pour in the sauce mixture and bring to a boil.

5. Return the beef to the wok, reduce the heat to medium, and simmer for 2 minutes. The sauce should coat the back of a spoon. Garnish with the scallions, and serve with the rice.

✳ Orange-Peel Beef

Tony orders this dish every time we eat Chinese food. It's sweet and spicy and delicious. The beef has a feather-light batter—not at all heavy or typical of many sweet-and-sour dishes. You can find dried orange peel at Asian markets, or order it online from www.penzeys.com. **Makes 4 servings**

1. Cutting against the grain, slice the beef as thinly as possible. In a medium bowl, whisk together the vinegar, 2 tablespoons of the peanut oil, and 2 tablespoons of the cornstarch until smooth. Add the beef and toss to coat. Cover tightly with plastic wrap and refrigerate for 30 minutes.

2. In a blender, combine the orange juice, chicken broth, lime juice, soy sauce, honey, sesame oil, and remaining 2 teaspoons of cornstarch. Blend until smooth.

3. Have all the ingredients ready before you start cooking. Heat a wok or large skillet over high heat until it starts to smoke, about 2 minutes. Reduce the heat to medium-high and add the remaining tablespoon of peanut oil. Swirl it around carefully, and add the beef. Sear the meat for 2 minutes, then transfer it to a plate. Add the orange peel, ginger, garlic, and chiles to the wok, stirring constantly, and cook for 30 seconds.

4. Add the sauce to the pan and bring to a boil, then reduce the heat to medium. Cook, stirring frequently, until the sauce thickens, 2 to 3 minutes. Return the beef to the pan, and add the scallions. Cook until the beef is hot, about 1 minute longer. Garnish with the fresh cilantro, and serve over rice.

1 1/2 pounds sirloin or flank steak

2 tablespoons rice wine vinegar

3 tablespoons peanut oil

2 tablespoons plus 2 teaspoons cornstarch

Freshly squeezed juice of 1 orange

1/4 cup low-sodium chicken broth or stock

Freshly squeezed juice of 1/2 lime

1 1/2 tablespoons soy sauce

1 tablespoon honey, or to taste

1 teaspoon toasted (Asian) sesame oil

2 (1-inch) strips dried orange peel

1 tablespoon minced ginger

1 teaspoon minced garlic

4 small dried hot chiles

4 scallions, trimmed and cut into 2-inch lengths

1 tablespoon finely chopped fresh cilantro

3 cups steamed brown or white rice

Churrasco con Chimichurri

2 pounds skirt steak

Kosher salt and freshly ground black pepper

For the chimichurri sauce:

1 bunch fresh flat-leaf parsley, finely chopped

1 bunch fresh cilantro, finely chopped

1/4 cup extra virgin olive oil

Juice of 2 freshly squeezed limes

1 tablespoon minced garlic

1 teaspoon dried oregano

3/4 teaspoon kosher salt

Pinch of crushed red pepper flakes

Corn or flour tortillas

I learned a lot about Latin cuisine when I lived in Miami. I remember taking Tony to an Argentinian restaurant where he fell in love with this classic dish. Loaded with garlic and herbs, the chimichurri sauce is delicious on everything: beef, chicken, pork, and even eggs. **Makes 6 servings**

1. Season both sides of the steak generously with salt and pepper.

2. In a small bowl, whisk together all the ingredients for the chimichurri sauce.

3. Heat a grill or a grill pan over medium-high heat. Grill the steaks, turning once, until medium-rare, about 3 minutes per side. Transfer to a cutting board, cover loosely with aluminum foil, and let rest for 5 minutes.

4. Slice the steak against the grain and serve with the sauce and warm corn or flour tortillas.

✳ Spice-Rubbed T-Bone

T-bone steak is a manly cut of beef; guys just love to gnaw on that bone. The peppery spice mix, seasoned with brown sugar, gives the T-bone an amazing caramelized and mouth-searing crust. If you like, you can serve this with a manly cocktail, like a classic martini. **Makes 4 servings**

1. Preheat the grill. Meanwhile, in a small bowl, combine all the spice rub ingredients and mix well.

2. Season the steaks generously with salt. Coat the steaks on both sides with the spice rub. Drizzle all over with the oil (if using).

3. Grill the steaks to the desired doneness, about 4 minutes per side for medium-rare.

Note: Chile de Arbol Long and slender in shape and deep red in color, dried chiles de arbol are used in Mexican cooking to add a grassy, smoky flavor to dishes. Used in powdered form to season soups and stews, chile de arbol can be purchased in Hispanic markets or online at www.myspicer.com.

For the spice rub:

2 tablespoons ancho chile powder (see note, page 35)

1 to 2 tablespoons brown sugar, to taste

1 tablespoon paprika

2 teaspoons freshly ground black pepper

2 teaspoons dried oregano

1 teaspoon ground coriander

1 teaspoon ground cumin

1 teaspoon ground chile de arbol (see note)

1/2 teaspoon ground cinnamon

4 (12-ounce) T-bone steaks, 1 inch thick

Kosher salt to taste

1 tablespoon chile oil, optional

Classic-tini

Makes 2 servings

1. Fill a shaker halfway with ice. Add the gin and stir for 1 minute.

2. Add ½ teaspoon of vermouth to each chilled martini glass. Strain the gin into the glasses. Garnish with 3 olives per glass, and serve immediately.

6 ounces premium gin

1 teaspoon dry vermouth

6 pimiento-stuffed olives

Filet Mignon with Red Wine Sauce

4 (6-ounce) filets mignons

Kosher salt and freshly ground black pepper

1½ tablespoons extra virgin olive oil

3 tablespoons minced shallot

1 teaspoon minced garlic

½ cup dry red wine

½ cup low-sodium chicken broth or stock

1 tablespoon cold unsalted butter

1 tablespoon chopped fresh flat-leaf parsley

1 tablespoon chopped fresh tarragon

Nothing beats perfectly cooked, tender filet mignon, especially when it's covered with an elegant red wine sauce. Tony and I love how the acidity from the wine sauce cuts the richness of the meat. I like to serve this with Two-Potato Gratin (page 145), but any potato recipe will work well with it. **Makes 4 servings**

1. Season the filets generously with salt and pepper all over. Heat a heavy-bottomed stainless-steel skillet over medium-high heat until very hot but not smoking, about 4 minutes.

2. Add the oil to the skillet, and then the filets, and cook them for about 4 minutes per side for medium-rare. Transfer the filets to a wire rack set over a warm plate. Tent the plate with foil and let them rest.

3. Return the pan to medium-high heat. Add the shallot, and cook, stirring, for 1 minute. Add the garlic, and cook, stirring, for 10 seconds more. Add the wine, bring to a boil, and simmer until it's reduced by a third, about 3 minutes. Pour in the broth and simmer until the sauce is syrupy and reduced, and coats the back of a spoon, about 6 minutes. Taste and adjust the seasoning if necessary.

4. Reduce the heat to medium and whisk in the butter and herbs, stirring constantly. Serve the filets drizzled with the sauce.

Filet with Sautéed Onions and Mushrooms

When Tony and I were dating back in college, this was the kind of dish I used to cook for him. Back then I used sirloin steak, which may not compare with filet for tenderness, but isn't too shabby for a college student. **Makes 4 servings**

1. Season the steaks generously on both sides with salt and pepper. Heat a large heavy-bottomed skillet over medium-high heat until very hot but not smoking, about 4 minutes. Add the oil and butter, then add the steaks and cook for 3 minutes per side. Transfer to a warm plate and tent it with foil to keep the steaks warm.

2. Add the onion to the pan and cook, stirring, until it begins to caramelize, about 4 minutes. Add the mushrooms and cook, stirring, until soft, about 3 minutes more. Add the garlic, and cook and stir for 30 seconds. Pour in the broth, and bring to a boil.

3. Reduce the heat to medium-high and cook until the sauce has thickened and reduced by half, about 5 minutes. Taste and adjust the seasoning if necessary. Return the steaks to the pan with the rosemary and cook for an additional 2 minutes for medium-rare. Serve immediately.

4 (8-ounce) filets mignons, about 1 3/4 inches thick

Kosher salt and freshly ground black pepper

1/2 tablespoon extra virgin olive oil

1/2 tablespoon unsalted butter

1 small red onion, thinly sliced

1 cup sliced button mushrooms

3 garlic cloves, thinly sliced

1 cup low-sodium chicken broth or stock

1 tablespoon chopped fresh rosemary

Beef Wellington
with Cabrales

8 (6-ounce) center-cut filets mignons, rinsed

Kosher salt and freshly ground black pepper

2 tablespoons extra virgin olive oil

4 tablespoons (1/2 stick) unsalted butter

2 cups thinly sliced onions

4 cups sliced wild mushrooms (such as cremini, shiitake, and oyster)

2 tablespoons minced garlic

Leaves from 4 sprigs fresh thyme

1 large egg

2 tablespoons whole milk

2 puff-pastry sheets, thawed

1/2 cup crumbled Cabrales or other blue cheese

This is the most elegant dish in the whole book. It also happens to be Tony's all-time favorite. Seared beef filets coated in sautéed wild mushrooms, caramelized onions, and blue cheese, then wrapped in puff pastry and baked—definitely a special-occasion dish (think birthday or anniversary). But it's worth all the effort, and the presentation is stunning! Cabrales is a Spanish blue cheese that Tony loves, but any blue cheese will be delicious here. I serve this knockout dish with Lobster Mashed Potatoes (page 144) for the ultimate surf 'n' turf experience. **Makes 8 servings**

1. Season the filets generously on both sides with salt and pepper. Place a large skillet over medium-high heat, and warm the oil until hot but not smoking. Add the filets, 4 at a time. Sear on both sides until brown, about 3 minutes per side. (You are not cooking the filets all the way through at this point.) Transfer to a plate and set aside. Repeat with the remaining filets. Cover tightly with plastic wrap and refrigerate until cold.

2. Using the same skillet, melt 2 tablespoons of the butter over medium heat, and add the onions. Cook, stirring frequently, until they are golden brown, 15 to 20 minutes. Transfer to a plate to cool, and set aside.

3. Using the same skillet, melt the remaining 2 tablespoons of butter over medium heat, and add the mushrooms. Cook, stirring frequently, until they have cooked down and released all of their juices, 10 to 15 minutes. Add the garlic, thyme, salt, and pepper, and cook for 1 minute. Transfer the mushrooms to a colander and let them drain for at least 15 minutes.

4. In a small bowl, whisk together the egg and milk. On a lightly floured surface, roll out the puff-pastry sheets into two 14-inch squares. Using a ruler to measure, trim the edges to form two 13-inch squares, then cut each square into four 6½-inch squares.

5. Place 1 tablespoon of Cabrales in the center of each pastry square and top with ⅛ of the mushroom mixture. Top the mushroom mixture with a filet, gently pressing down. Top the filet with ⅛ of the caramelized onions. Wrap two opposite corners of the puff pastry over the onions, overlapping them. Seal the seam with the egg wash. Wrap the remaining corners of pastry over the filet and seal in the same manner. Seal any gaps with the egg wash and press the pastry around the filet to enclose it completely. Repeat with the remaining ingredients.

6. Transfer the wrapped filets, seam side down, to a parchment-lined baking sheet. Chill the remaining egg wash. Chill the beef Wellingtons, loosely covered, for at least 2 hours or up to 1 day.

7. Preheat the oven to 425° F. Brush the beef Wellingtons all over with the egg wash. Bake, uncovered, 20 to 30 minutes, until the pastry is golden brown and a meat thermometer inserted in the center of the filets registers 120° F. Let the Wellingtons rest for 10 minutes, then cut in half to display the layers. Serve with Lobster Mashed Potatoes.

✳ Beef Tournedos with Corn and Chipotle

8 (3-ounce) beef tournedos

Kosher salt and freshly ground black pepper

1 tablespoon extra virgin olive oil

2 1/2 cups fresh or frozen corn kernels (from 2 to 3 ears of corn)

1/4 cup chopped shallot

1/4 cup chopped red bell pepper

1/4 cup chopped yellow bell pepper

1 teaspoon minced garlic

2/3 cup diced tomatoes

2/3 cup low-sodium chicken broth or stock

1/4 teaspoon ground chipotle chile (see note, page 35)

1 tablespoon unsalted butter

1/3 cup minced fresh cilantro

1/4 cup chopped scallions

In 1997, Tony's second year in the league, I started making this dish, and he's been crazy about it ever since. Tournedos are thin slices of beef tenderloin, which cook up quickly and stay very tender if you don't overcook them. The ground chipotle gives the beef a great spicy kick and plays off the sweetness of the corn. It's a fairly light combination for a beef dish, so it's the kind of dish I like to make in the summer, when I can get fresh corn and really good tomatoes. But Tony's happy to eat it all year long. **Makes 4 servings**

1. Heat a large nonstick skillet over medium-high heat. Season the tournedos on both sides with salt and pepper. Add the oil to the skillet. Working in batches, sear the steaks on both sides, 1 minute per side, then transfer them to a plate and tent it with foil to keep them warm.

2. Add the corn kernels to the hot pan and cook until some of the kernels begin to brown, 3 to 5 minutes. Reduce the heat to medium. Add the shallot, red and yellow peppers, and the garlic, and cook, stirring, for 3 more minutes. Add the tomatoes, broth, and chipotle pepper, and season with salt. Bring to a boil. Reduce the heat to medium and simmer for 5 minutes.

3. Taste and adjust the seasoning if necessary. Stir in the butter and return the steaks to the pan. Reduce the heat to low and cook for 3 minutes, until the steaks are heated through. Place 2 tournedos of beef on each plate and top them with the corn mixture. Garnish with cilantro and scallions.

Pleasing Pork, Veal, Lamb, and Venison

Perfect Panko-Crusted Pork Chops

1/2 cup all-purpose flour

Kosher salt and freshly ground black pepper

2 cups panko bread crumbs (see note, page 19)

2 large eggs, lightly beaten

2 tablespoons whole milk

4 bone-in center loin pork chops, 1 inch thick

1 tablespoon Cajun seasoning (see note, page 54)

3 tablespoons canola oil

These are the lightest, crispiest pork chops ever, thanks to the panko bread crumbs. They remind Tony of the fried pork chops his mother made when he was a kid, so I make them for him on a regular basis. The combination of browning them on the stove and then finishing them in the oven keeps the meat juicy and tender, yet ensures they will be cooked through. This recipe works equally well with veal chops.

Makes 4 servings

1. Preheat the oven to 350° F. Place the flour in a shallow dish and season with salt and pepper. Place the bread crumbs in a separate shallow dish and season with salt and pepper. Combine the eggs and milk in another shallow dish and season with salt and pepper. Season the pork chops with the Cajun seasoning.

2. Dredge the pork chops in the flour and shake off the excess. Next, dip the chops in the egg mixture. Finally, dredge the chops in the bread crumbs, pressing on them to help the crumbs adhere.

3. Heat a large cast-iron skillet or other large frying pan over medium-high heat and add the oil. When the oil is hot but not smoking, add the pork chops and cook until golden, about 4 minutes. Turn them and reduce the heat to medium. Cook until the pork is golden brown on the second side, about 6 more minutes.

4. Transfer the pan to the oven and bake until just cooked through, about 5 minutes.

5. Remove the pan from the oven and place the pork chops on paper-towel-lined plates to drain. Serve immediately.

Seared Veal Chops with Thyme and Rosemary

I think serving bone-in meat harks back to caveman days—but you've got to give your man what he wants. Tony wants veal with the bone in, so that's what he gets. The lemon zest gives the veal a citrusy bite that works tremendously well with the herbs. **Makes 4 servings**

1. Place the veal chops in a shallow dish. In a small bowl, combine the oil, thyme, rosemary, garlic, and lemon zest, and pour the mixture over the veal, turning the chops to coat. Cover the dish tightly with plastic wrap and marinate in the refrigerator for 4 to 8 hours.

2. Heat a grill pan or cast-iron skillet over medium-high heat for 3 minutes. Remove the veal chops from the marinade and brush off the clinging bits of garlic. Season the chops generously with salt and pepper.

3. Grill the chops, turning once, until cooked through, about 5 minutes per side for medium. Transfer the chops to a plate and serve.

4 bone-in veal chops, 1 inch thick

3 tablespoons extra virgin olive oil

2 tablespoons finely chopped fresh thyme

2 tablespoons finely chopped fresh rosemary

4 garlic cloves, minced

2 teaspoons finely grated lemon zest

Kosher salt and freshly ground black pepper

Veal Scaloppine

1/4 cup all-purpose flour

Kosher salt

Freshly ground black pepper

3 tablespoons extra virgin olive oil

4 (6-ounce) boneless veal chops, pounded very thin (see note, page 99)

2 garlic cloves, thinly sliced

1/2 cup dry white wine

1 cup low-sodium chicken broth or stock

Freshly squeezed juice and finely grated zest of 1 lemon

1/2 cup chopped fresh flat-leaf parsley

5 fresh sage leaves, cut into a chiffonade (see note, page 32)

1 pound pasta, cooked according to package instructions

My version of veal scaloppine is different from most. Instead of buying presliced scaloppine (usually cut from the leg of the calf), I pound boneless veal chops until they are very thin, as this cut is much more tender. The scaloppines cook in a flash, and the quick light sauce dresses both the meat and the pasta. Sage adds a wonderful bit of earthiness.

Makes 4 servings

1. In a shallow bowl, combine the flour with 1½ teaspoons of salt and ½ teaspoon of pepper. In a 12-inch sauté pan over high heat, warm the oil. Dredge the veal chops in the seasoned flour, shaking off the excess. Place 2 chops in the pan and cook, turning once, until browned, about 2 minutes per side. Transfer the chops to a plate and repeat with the remaining chops.

2. Reduce the heat to medium, add the garlic to the pan, and cook, stirring, for 15 seconds. Pour the wine into the pan, and bring to a boil, stirring and scraping up the browned bits from the bottom of the pan. Simmer until the wine is syrupy and reduced by half. Add the chicken broth, lemon juice, and lemon zest, and bring to a boil. Cook until the sauce begins to thicken, 3 to 4 minutes.

3. Season with salt and pepper to taste. Return the veal to the pan and simmer until cooked through, about 1 minute. Add the parsley and sage. Transfer the veal to a platter. Pour the sauce over the veal and serve immediately, over hot pasta.

Veal Marsala with Mushrooms

Veal Marsala with mushrooms is a classic. I stick to the basic recipe, but use earthy cremini mushrooms for added flavor. Combined with the sweetness of Marsala wine, it's an ideal complement to the veal. As in my veal scaloppine recipe, I prefer to pound boneless veal chops rather than buy precut scaloppine, since the scaloppine you buy can be tough and easy to overcook. Pounded chops are much more tender, and worth the little bit of extra work. **Makes 4 servings**

1. In a large dish, combine the flour, 1½ teaspoons of the salt, and ½ teaspoon of the pepper and mix well. Dredge the veal chops in the seasoned flour, shaking off the excess. In a large skillet over medium-high heat, warm the oil. Place 2 of the veal chops in the pan and cook, turning once, until browned, about 1 minute per side. Transfer the chops to a plate and repeat with the other 2 chops.

2. Reduce the heat to medium, add the garlic and mushrooms, and cook, stirring, until soft, 3 to 5 minutes. Pour the broth and Marsala into the pan and bring to a boil, scraping up any browned bits with a wooden spoon. Simmer until the liquid reduces by half, 10 to 15 minutes. Taste and adjust the seasoning if necessary.

3. Whisk the butter into the sauce, and return the veal to the pan. Add the parsley and cook until the veal is heated through, about 2 minutes. Remove the veal from the heat and serve immediately, over hot pasta.

1/4 cup all-purpose flour

1 1/2 teaspoons kosher salt, plus additional

1/2 teaspoon freshly ground black pepper, plus additional

4 (6-ounce) boneless veal chops, pounded very thin (see note, page 99)

2 tablespoons extra virgin olive oil

1 teaspoon minced garlic

1 pound cremini mushrooms, sliced

1 cup low-sodium chicken broth or stock

3/4 cup Marsala wine

1 tablespoon unsalted butter

1 tablespoon chopped fresh flat-leaf parsley

1 pound pasta, cooked according to package instructions

# Veal Saltimbocca

4 (8-ounce) bone-in veal rib chops, preferably frenched (have your butcher do this for you)

Kosher salt and freshly ground black pepper

2 tablespoons extra virgin olive oil

8 whole sage leaves

8 slices imported prosciutto, thinly sliced

4 ounces Fontina cheese, cut into 4 slices

Tony's favorite veal dish ever! I introduced it to him when we lived in St. Louis. We were out to dinner with a group of quarterbacks and their wives, and I ordered it (of course I was the only woman to order it; all the others got salad and fish). Tony had one taste and it was love at first bite. Serve with Wild Mushroom Risotto (page 79). **Makes 4 servings**

1. Season the veal chops on both sides with salt and pepper. Heat a large ovenproof skillet over medium-high heat. When hot but not smoking, add the oil and veal chops. Sear the chops, turning once, until browned, about 2 minutes per side. Transfer to a plate and let rest until cool enough to handle.

2. Preheat the oven to 450° F. Lay 2 sage leaves on top of each chop. Wrap each chop inside 2 slices of prosciutto, covering only the meat, not the bone.

3. Return the prosciutto-wrapped veal to the pan and roast until done to taste, about 8 to 10 minutes for medium, depending on the thickness of the chops. Remove the chops from the oven and preheat the broiler. Top each chop with cheese and broil until the cheese has melted, about 1 minute.

✳ Herb-and-Garlic-Crusted Rack of Lamb
with Mint Sauce

Rack of lamb with garlic is a classic, and so is serving lamb with mint sauce. I've combined the two here for a gutsy dish that will appeal to anyone who likes meat with plenty of flavor. Like Tony. **Makes 8 servings**

1. In a small bowl, stir together the bread crumbs, oil, basil, rosemary, thyme, mint, garlic, and 1 teaspoon of the salt until well-combined.

2. Generously season the lamb racks with salt and pepper on both sides. Heat a roasting pan over two burners on medium-high heat.

3. Place the racks, fat side down, in the hot pan, and sear the lamb, turning once, until browned, 2 to 3 minutes per side. Transfer the racks to a plate and let cool for 15 minutes. (The racks can be prepared a day ahead, cooled completely, wrapped, and refrigerated at this point. To finish, bring the lamb to room temperature before crusting.)

4. While the lamb is cooling, preheat the oven to 400° F. Line a baking sheet with parchment paper. Once the lamb has cooled, brush the fat side of the racks with 1 tablespoon of mustard per rack. Using your hands, coat each rack with half of the bread-crumb mixture, covering everything but the bones. (Crust the fat side only.)

5. Set a wire rack over a rimmed baking sheet. Place the lamb, fat side up, on the rack and roast to desired doneness, 20 to 25 minutes for medium-rare. Let them rest on a cutting board for 10 minutes, tented with foil. Cut each rack into chops.

6. To make the mint sauce, combine the mint, honey, lime juice, and garlic in a blender and blend until smooth. To serve, spoon some mint sauce in the center of each plate and top with 2 chops.

3/4 cup panko bread crumbs (see note, page 19)

2 tablespoons extra virgin olive oil

2 tablespoons chopped fresh basil

1 tablespoon chopped fresh rosemary

1 tablespoon chopped fresh thyme

1 tablespoon chopped fresh mint

1 tablespoon minced garlic

1 teaspoon kosher salt, plus additional

2 racks of lamb, trimmed and Frenched (have your butcher do this for you)

2 teaspoons freshly ground black pepper

2 tablespoons Dijon mustard

For the mint sauce:
2 cups fresh mint leaves
3 tablespoons honey
Freshly squeezed juice of 1 lime
1 garlic clove, minced

Herb-Roasted Leg of Lamb

with New Potatoes

10 garlic cloves, chopped

10 sprigs fresh lemon thyme, chopped

6 sprigs fresh rosemary, chopped

1 tablespoon minced ginger

Kosher salt

Freshly ground black pepper

Freshly squeezed juice and finely grated zest of 2 lemons

1/4 cup low-sodium soy sauce

1/4 cup extra virgin olive oil

2 teaspoons toasted (Asian) sesame oil

1 (7-pound) leg of lamb, partially boned and tied (have your butcher do this for you)

3 pounds new potatoes, cut into 1-inch pieces

1/4 cup chopped fresh flat-leaf parsley

I love serving leg of lamb for company. It's always a pretty reasonably priced cut of meat, which is good when you are serving a crowd, and you end up with parts that are medium-rare and medium, so it appeals to everyone. Tony is a sucker for this dish because it is so juicy and succulent. I like to serve it with something green, like Sautéed Swiss Chard with Balsamic Vinegar (page 140). **Makes 8 servings**

1. Using a mortar and pestle, pulverize the garlic, thyme, rosemary, ginger, 1½ teaspoons salt, and 1 teaspoon pepper together until somewhat smooth. Add the lemon juice and zest, soy sauce, 2 table-spoons of the olive oil, and the sesame oil, and stir well to combine.

2. With the tip of a paring knife, cut small slits all over the lamb. Place the lamb in a large bowl or a resealable plastic bag and pour the marinade over it, turning to coat. Cover the bowl tightly with plastic wrap, transfer to the refrigerator, and marinate at least 8 hours or overnight.

3. Preheat the oven to 450° F. In a large roasting pan, toss the potatoes with the remaining 2 tablespoons of the olive oil, and season with salt and pepper. Arrange the potatoes in a single layer on the bottom of the pan. Season the lamb with salt and pepper. Place the lamb on top of the potatoes and roast, uncovered, for 20 minutes.

4. Reduce the heat to 350° F. Continue to roast, stirring the potatoes occasionally, until a meat thermometer inserted into the thickest part of the lamb (do not touch the bone) registers 135° F for medium, 50 to 60 minutes.

5. Transfer the lamb to a cutting board and let it rest for 10 minutes before carving. To serve, place some potatoes in the center of each plate. Top with several slices of lamb, garnish with the fresh parsley, and drizzle the pan juices on top. Serve hot.

✳ Pecan-Crusted Venison

I love cooking meats with a crust because it not only adds a crisp texture, it's also a great place to sneak in some extra flavor. In this dish, the pecans lend crunch while the garlic, oregano, and marjoram give it an Italian accent. Boiled or roasted new potatoes are the perfect accompaniment.

Makes 6 servings

- 1 cup finely ground pecans
- 1/2 cup fresh bread crumbs
- 2 tablespoons extra virgin olive oil
- 2 tablespoons chopped fresh flat-leaf parsley
- 1 tablespoon roasted garlic paste (see box, page 10)
- 1 teaspoon dried oregano
- 1 teaspoon dried marjoram
- Kosher salt and freshly ground black pepper
- 1 (3- to 5-pound) boneless venison roast, trimmed and tied with butcher twine

1. Preheat the oven to 425° F.

2. In a small bowl, stir together the pecans, bread crumbs, oil, parsley, garlic paste, oregano, marjoram, salt, and pepper. Season the venison generously with salt and pepper. Coat the venison with the nut mixture on all sides, pressing on the crust to help it adhere. Transfer the roast to a rack set over a rimmed baking sheet.

3. Roast until a meat thermometer registers at least 125° F, 8 to 12 minutes per pound, depending on desired doneness. Set the pan aside to rest for 10 minutes. Remove the twine, slice the meat, and serve.

Tex-Mex Venison
with Spicy Cranberry Sauce

For the spicy cranberry sauce:

1 tablespoon unsalted butter

1 tablespoon finely chopped shallot

1 tablespoon roasted garlic paste (see box, page 10)

1 teaspoon minced serrano chile pepper

1/2 cup port wine

1/2 cup low-sodium chicken broth or stock

1/2 cup cranberry juice

1 tablespoon honey

1/2 cup dried cranberries

Kosher salt and freshly ground black pepper

1 teaspoon ground cumin

1 teaspoon ground coriander

1 teaspoon ancho chile powder (see note, page 35)

6 (4- to 6-ounce) bone-in venison rib chops

Kosher salt and freshly ground black pepper

2 tablespoons extra virgin olive oil

Venison, like lamb, is one of those kinds of meat that can stand up to as much spice as you want to give it. So here I don't hold back on the chile in the seasonings. Since I think fruit and game are superb together, I like to serve the venison with a zesty dried-cranberry sauce that is spicy, tart, sweet, and rich at the same time. It's another of Tony's all-time favorites. If you can, make the cranberry sauce a day or two ahead; it's even better when the flavors have had a chance to come together. **Makes 6 servings**

1. To prepare the cranberry sauce, in a small saucepan over medium heat, melt the butter. Add the shallot, garlic paste, and serrano pepper, and sauté until softened, about 5 minutes. Raise the heat to medium-high. Add the port, bring to a boil, and simmer until the liquid is reduced to 2 tablespoons, about 5 minutes.

2. Add the broth, cranberry juice, and honey to the pan, and continue to simmer until the sauce is reduced by a third, about 7 minutes. Strain the sauce through a fine sieve, return it to the pan, and set the pan over low heat. Add the dried cranberries and cook until they soften slightly, about 5 minutes. Taste and adjust the seasoning if necessary.

3. To prepare the venison, in a small bowl, combine the cumin, coriander, and chile powder. Season the venison chops on both sides with salt, pepper, and the spice mixture.

4. Heat a large sauté pan over medium-high heat. Add the oil, and sauté the venison for 3 minutes per side. Serve with the cranberry sauce.

Simply Side Dishes

Sautéed Spinach with Garlic

Steamed Broccolini

Green Beans with Toasted Pine Nuts

"Pickled" Red Cabbage

Sautéed Swiss Chard with Balsamic Vinegar

Roasted Corn with Old Bay Butter

Maque Choux

Mashed Sweet Potatoes

Lobster Mashed Potatoes

Two-Potato Gratin

Sweet Plantains (Maduros)

Spiced Basmati Rice Pilaf

Jasmine Mango Rice Pilaf

Cumin Rice

Quick Red Beans and Rice

Sautéed Spinach with Garlic

1½ tablespoons extra virgin olive oil

4 garlic cloves, thinly sliced

2 pounds fresh baby spinach

Kosher salt and freshly ground black pepper

½ tablespoon freshly squeezed lemon juice

This is a very simple, savory recipe that takes about five minutes to make if you buy prewashed baby spinach in a bag. It goes with almost anything, so serve it anytime you want to have a delicious green vegetable on the side. And, of course, spinach is so good for you. **Makes 4 servings**

1. Heat a very large skillet or stockpot over medium-high heat for 2 minutes. Add the oil and garlic and cook until lightly browned, about 1 minute.

2. Stir in the spinach in batches, adding more as it wilts. Season with salt and pepper and cook, stirring, until all the spinach is slightly wilted, 2 to 3 minutes. Drizzle with the lemon juice and serve hot.

✳ Steamed Broccolini

Broccolini, a trademarked cross between broccoli and Chinese kale, is sweet, quick to cook, and very flavorful. Here, I just season it with chicken broth, some chile, and a little bit of garlic. It's a substantial side dish but very light at the same time, and goes with almost anything, from meat and poultry to seafood or even pasta—if you want something green other than a salad. **Makes 4 servings**

1 tablespoon extra virgin olive oil

1 teaspoon minced garlic

Pinch of crushed red pepper flakes

2 pounds broccolini, stem ends removed

1 tablespoon low-sodium chicken broth or stock

Kosher salt and freshly ground black pepper

1. Heat a large saucepan over medium-high heat. Add the oil, garlic, and crushed red pepper, and cook, stirring, for 30 seconds. Add the broccolini and chicken broth, and season with salt and pepper. Cover and reduce the heat to medium.

2. Cook, shaking the pan to ensure even cooking, until tender, 3 to 5 minutes.

# Green Beans with Toasted Pine Nuts

Kosher salt

2 pounds fresh green beans, trimmed

2 tablespoons extra virgin olive oil

1 teaspoon minced garlic

1 tablespoon low-sodium chicken broth or stock

Freshly ground black pepper

1/2 cup pine nuts, toasted (see note)

Tony, the texture guy, likes his green beans on the crisp side, and I completely agree. To ensure that, I quickly blanch the beans, then stop the cooking by plunging them in ice water. At the last minute I warm them up with the nuts, a little garlic, chicken broth, and olive oil. They've got great flavor as well as crunch. **Makes 8 servings**

1. Bring a large pot of salted water to a boil. Fill a bowl with ice water. Add the beans to the boiling water and cook until just tender, 2 to 3 minutes. Drain the beans, and immediately transfer them to the ice water to stop the cooking, then drain them again.

2. In a large saucepan over medium heat, warm the oil. Add the garlic and cook, stirring, for 30 seconds. Add the beans and chicken broth, and season with salt and pepper. Cover, and cook until the beans are warm, about 3 minutes.

3. Stir in the pine nuts and serve warm or at room temperature.

Note: Toasting Pine Nuts To toast the pine nuts, heat them in a small saucepan over medium heat, shaking the pan occasionally so that they toast evenly. Toast the nuts until golden and fragrant, watching carefully to see that they do not burn, 6 to 8 minutes. Transfer them immediately to a plate.

✳ "Pickled" Red Cabbage

I usually serve this "pickled" cabbage with my fish tacos, but it's also great with grilled meats, chicken, or on its own as a snack. If you have tongs, use them to turn and toss the cabbage. They are easier to use than a spoon or spatula for this.

Makes 10 servings

2 tablespoons canola oil

1 head red cabbage, cored and thinly sliced

1/4 cup red wine vinegar

3 tablespoons sugar

Kosher salt and freshly ground black pepper

1. In a large saucepan over medium-high heat, warm the oil. Add the cabbage and cook, stirring, until it begins to wilt, 3 to 5 minutes.

2. Reduce the heat to medium, stir in the vinegar and sugar, and season with salt and pepper. Cover the pan and cook until the cabbage has wilted significantly but still has a slight crunch, about 5 minutes.

# Sautéed Swiss Chard with Balsamic Vinegar

1 tablespoon extra virgin
   olive oil

1 teaspoon minced garlic

4 small or 2 large bunches
   Swiss chard (preferably
   red), stems removed,
   leaves torn

2 tablespoons low-sodium
   chicken broth or stock

2 teaspoons balsamic vinegar

Kosher salt and freshly
   ground black pepper

Swiss chard is an extremely easy vegetable to grow in your garden, even in the hot Texas sun. In the summer I typically have a huge harvest of it, and this is Tony's favorite way to eat it. **Makes 4 servings**

1. In a large skillet over medium-high heat, warm the oil. Add the garlic and cook, stirring, until fragrant, about 20 seconds. Add the Swiss chard, chicken broth, vinegar, and salt and pepper to taste.

2. Continue to cook the leaves, tossing gently, until they are slightly wilted, about 5 minutes. Serve immediately.

Roasted Corn with Old Bay Butter

Roasting or grilling is my favorite method of cooking corn. While living in Baltimore for two years, I cooked with the town's seasoning of choice, Old Bay, and I came up with this unique way to use it. The seasoning mix gives the corn a nice spicy, salty, flavorful kick. **Makes 6 servings**

6 ears fresh corn

4 tablespoons (1/2 stick) unsalted butter, softened

1 teaspoon Old Bay seasoning

1. Soak the corn, husks on, in water for 30 minutes. Peel back the husks, remove the silk, and re-cover the corn with the husks.

2. Preheat the oven to 400° F. Place the corn directly on the oven rack. Cook for 30 minutes, turning halfway through the cooking time.

3. While the corn cooks, combine the butter and seasoning in a small bowl and mix well.

4. Peel the husks and spread a dollop of butter on each cob. Serve hot.

Maque Choux

1/2 pound bacon, chopped

4 ears fresh corn

1 cup chopped onions

1/2 cup chopped red bell pepper

1/2 cup chopped green bell pepper

1 bay leaf

1 teaspoon Cajun seasoning (see note, page 54)

1 teaspoon dried thyme

1/4 teaspoon cayenne pepper

Kosher salt and freshly ground black pepper

1/2 cup heavy cream

1/4 cup chopped scallions

1/4 cup chopped fresh flat-leaf parsley

Maque choux is a classic Creole side dish loaded with corn and peppers. Often, it also has lima beans in it, which is one of the only beans Tony dislikes. That is why you don't see them in this dish, but you can add some if you like them.

Makes 4 servings

1. In a large skillet over medium-high heat, cook the bacon until crisp, 4 to 6 minutes. Use a slotted spoon to transfer the bacon to a paper-towel-lined plate to drain. Pour off all but 2 tablespoons of the fat in the pan.

2. Working over a bowl, cut the corn kernels off the cob. Using the back of a large knife, scrape the cob twice to release the milk, adding this liquid to the corn.

3. Place the skillet over medium heat. Add the onions and the bell peppers, and cook, stirring, until soft, 6 to 8 minutes. Add the corn and its milk, the bay leaf, Cajun seasoning, thyme, and cayenne, and season with salt and pepper. Cook for 5 minutes, stirring occasionally.

4. Reduce the heat to low, stirring in the reserved bacon, the cream, scallions, and the parsley. Cook until the cream is absorbed, 3 to 5 minutes. Discard the bay leaf. Taste and adjust the seasoning if necessary.

Mashed Sweet Potatoes

These lovely mashed sweet potatoes are like a pie without the crust. Baking the potatoes instead of the usual boiling method makes them very creamy and delicious to begin with, and they're even better mixed with cinnamon and brown sugar. **Makes 4 servings**

2 pounds sweet potatoes, pricked all over with a fork

2 tablespoons unsalted butter, optional

2 tablespoons brown sugar

1 teaspoon ground cinnamon

1. Preheat the oven to 450° F. Place the whole, unpeeled potatoes in a single layer on a piece of aluminum foil directly on the oven rack. Bake the potatoes until they are very soft, 45 minutes to 1 hour, depending on their size.

2. Allow the potatoes to cool until they can be handled easily, about 15 minutes. Using a knife, remove the skin from the potatoes, and place them in a bowl or the bowl of a food processor. Add the butter (if using) and the brown sugar and cinnamon. Using a potato masher or the food processor, mash the potatoes until they are smooth and creamy. Serve hot.

Lobster Mashed Potatoes

2 pounds new potatoes,
    peeled and cubed

3/4 cup low-fat buttermilk,
    warmed, plus additional if
    necessary

3 tablespoons unsalted butter

1 tablespoon roasted garlic
    paste (see box, page 10)

Kosher salt and freshly
    ground black pepper

1 pound cooked lobster meat,
    roughly chopped (see note)

I like to serve this with Beef Wellington with Cabrales (page 122) for my take on surf 'n' turf. In the same vein, they are also great with any grilled meat. You could substitute shrimp for the lobster, but the lobster makes it very special.

Makes 6 servings

1. Bring a large pot of salted water to a boil over high heat. Add the potatoes and cook until fork-tender, 15 to 20 minutes. Drain well.

2. Pass the potatoes through a ricer or use a masher to mash them to the desired consistency. Return the potatoes to the hot pan and stir in the buttermilk, 2 tablespoons of the butter, and the garlic paste, and season with salt and pepper. (If the potato mixture is too thick, stir in a little more buttermilk.) Cover to keep warm.

3. In a small saucepan over medium-high heat, melt the remaining tablespoon of butter. Add the lobster meat and salt and pepper to taste, and cook, stirring, until the lobster is warm, about 3 minutes. Fold the sautéed lobster meat into the potatoes, taste, adjust the seasoning if necessary, and serve hot.

Note: One whole lobster or lobster tail usually equals about ½ pound of shelled meat, so you'll need two here.

Two-Potato Gratin

My mom used to make mean potatoes au gratin when I was a kid. I tweaked the recipe, adding sweet potatoes and jalapeño Jack cheese to give it a little something extra. My mom always used Yukon Gold potatoes for their creaminess and so do I. **Makes 8 servings**

1. Preheat the oven to 400° F. Butter a square gratin dish or an 8-inch square baking dish with the butter.

2. In a small saucepan over medium heat, bring the heavy cream and garlic just to a simmer. Simmer gently until slightly thickened, about 10 minutes.

3. Arrange a layer of sweet potatoes on the bottom of the dish, and sprinkle with salt, pepper, ¼ of the onion, and ¼ cup of each cheese.

4. Repeat with a layer of the Yukon Gold potatoes, again sprinkling evenly with salt, pepper, ¼ of the onion, and ¼ cup of each cheese. Repeat, alternating layers, and ending with the last of the cheese.

5. Pour the hot cream mixture over the potatoes and top with foil. Bake, covered, until fork-tender, 45 to 55 minutes. Remove the foil and bake for an additional 10 minutes, or until the gratin is golden brown on top. Allow the gratin to cool for 10 minutes before serving.

1 tablespoon unsalted butter

2 cups heavy cream

2 garlic cloves, minced

1 pound sweet potatoes, scrubbed and cut into 1/4-inch rounds

Kosher salt and freshly ground black pepper

1/2 small yellow onion, thinly sliced

1 cup grated sharp white Cheddar cheese

1 cup grated jalapeño Jack cheese

1 pound Yukon Gold potatoes, scrubbed and cut into 1/4-inch rounds

Sweet Plantains
(Maduros)

3 large plantains, ripened until their skins turn black

3 tablespoons unsalted butter, or more as necessary

fell in love with maduros when I lived in Miami. There was a place around the corner from my apartment that made them and I was hooked! When I left Miami, I tried to replicate them, and it took several tries to get it right. I learned that the plantains have to be very ripe, almost too ripe, for them to be soft and sweet. So look for plantains that are black all over. Or buy yellow speckled ones ahead of time and let them ripen for a few days before making this. It really makes all the difference. **Makes 8 servings**

1. To peel the plantains, cut the ends off and discard. Using a sharp knife, make 2 long cuts lengthwise through the skin, and remove the peel. Cut the plantains into ¼-inch-thick rounds.

2. In a large nonstick skillet over medium-low heat, melt the butter.

3. Add the plantains to the pan in one layer and cook in batches, adding more butter if necessary. Turn the plantains frequently and adjust the heat so as not to burn them. Cook until golden brown and tender, 8 to 10 minutes. Serve hot.

✳ Spiced Basmati Rice Pilaf

Flavored with spices like cardamom, cumin, and ginger, this Indian-inspired rice dish is tastier than your average pilaf, but not any harder to make. It's great with pork, chicken, and fish. **Makes 6 servings**

1. Place the rice in a colander and rinse under cold running water until the water runs clear. Allow the rice to drain in the colander for 30 minutes.

2. Heat the oil in a large saucepan over medium-high heat. Add the shallot and sauté until soft, about 2 minutes. Add the garlic and cook 30 seconds more. Stir in the cinnamon, ginger, cardamom, cumin, and bay leaf, and cook an additional 30 seconds, or until fragrant.

3. Add the rice and cook, stirring constantly, until the rice begins to brown, about 5 minutes. Add the broth and bring to a boil. Cover the pan and reduce the heat to low. Cook the rice until all the liquid is absorbed, 15 to 20 minutes.

4. Remove the rice from the heat and let it stand, covered, for 10 minutes. Discard the bay leaf. Taste and adjust the seasoning if necessary. Stir in the parsley and serve hot.

2 cups basmati rice

2 tablespoons canola oil

1 small shallot, minced

2 garlic cloves, minced

1/2 teaspoon ground cinnamon

1/2 teaspoon ground ginger

1/2 teaspoon ground cardamom

1/2 teaspoon ground cumin

1 bay leaf

4 cups low-sodium chicken broth or stock

1/4 cup chopped fresh flat-leaf parsley

Jasmine Mango Rice Pilaf

2 cups jasmine rice

3 tablespoons unsalted butter

1 cup chopped onions

4 cups low-sodium chicken broth or stock

2 cups diced mango (from 2 to 3 ripe mangoes)

2 bay leaves

Mangoes are my all-time favorite fruit, and I love their tart sweetness combined with fragrant, floral jasmine rice. It's a different and divine pilaf that everyone you serve it to will remember. Try pairing this with Sesame-Crusted Mahi-Mahi (page 84). **Makes 8 servings**

1. Place the rice in a colander and rinse under cold running water until the water runs clear. Allow the rice to drain in the colander for 30 minutes.

2. In a large saucepan over medium heat, melt the butter. Add the onions and cook until very soft, 5 to 7 minutes. Add the rice and cook, stirring constantly, until the rice begins to brown, about 5 minutes.

3. Stir in the broth, mango, and bay leaves, and bring the mixture to a boil. Cover and reduce the heat to low. Cook until all the liquid is absorbed, 15 to 20 minutes. Remove the pan from the heat and let it stand, covered, for a few minutes. Discard the bay leaves. Serve hot.

Cumin Rice

Since I'm not a big fan of plain rice, I add a little cumin and coriander to this recipe. Cumin is probably my favorite spice, and it works really well here with the buttery, toasted rice and the hint of coriander. If you don't use your ground cumin and coriander seeds as often as I do, and they've been hanging out in the cabinet for more than a year, buy fresh jars before making this. It's worth it. **Makes 6 servings**

1 tablespoon unsalted butter

1 tablespoon extra virgin olive oil

2 tablespoons minced shallot

1 teaspoon minced garlic

1/2 cup minced fresh cilantro

2 teaspoons ground cumin

1 teaspoon coriander seeds, crushed

1 1/2 cups jasmine or basmati rice, rinsed

2 1/2 cups low-sodium chicken broth or stock

Kosher salt and freshly ground black pepper

1 tablespoon freshly squeezed lime juice

1. In a medium saucepan over medium heat, melt the butter with the olive oil. Add the shallot and garlic and cook until fragrant, about 2 minutes. Add ¼ cup of the cilantro, the cumin, and the coriander, and cook for 30 seconds more.

2. Add the rice and cook, stirring to coat, for an additional 2 minutes. Pour in the broth, season with salt and pepper, and bring to a boil. Cover the pan and reduce the heat to low. Cook until all the liquid is absorbed, 15 to 20 minutes.

3. Remove the pan from the heat and let it stand, covered, for 10 minutes. Stir in the remaining cilantro and the lime juice. Taste and adjust the seasoning if necessary. Serve hot.

Quick Red Beans and Rice

1 tablespoon extra virgin olive oil

6 ounces andouille sausage, diced (see note, page 47)

1 cup chopped onions

1/2 cup chopped green bell pepper

2 teaspoons minced garlic

1 teaspoon dried thyme

1/2 teaspoon Cajun seasoning (see note, page 54)

1/4 teaspoon cayenne pepper

1 bay leaf

1 cup long-grain white rice

2 cups low-sodium chicken broth or stock

1 (15-ounce) can red beans, rinsed and drained

1/4 cup chopped scallions

1/4 cup chopped fresh flat-leaf parsley

1 teaspoon Louisiana hot sauce (such as Crystal or Frank's)

Although great as a hearty side, this spicy, sausage-filled Cajun dish is traditionally served as a meal in itself. When we lived in St. Louis, Tony used to ask me to make this about once a week. **Makes 6 servings**

1. In a large saucepan over medium-high heat, warm the oil. Add the sausage and cook, stirring occasionally, until brown on all sides, 4 to 6 minutes. Reduce the heat to medium, add the onions and bell pepper, and cook, stirring, until soft, about 5 minutes.

2. Add the garlic, thyme, Cajun seasoning, cayenne, and bay leaf, and cook, stirring, until fragrant, about 30 seconds. Add the rice and cook, stirring to coat, for 1 minute. Raise the heat to high, stir in the broth and beans, and bring to a boil. Reduce the heat to low and cover. Cook until all the liquid is absorbed, 15 to 20 minutes.

3. Taste the rice-and-bean mixture and adjust the seasoning if necessary. Discard the bay leaf. Add the scallions, parsley, and hot sauce, and serve hot.

Bye-Week Brunch

Girl Scout Camp French Toast

Light-as-a-Feather Pancakes

Whole Wheat Pancakes

Chocolate Waffles

Uncle D's Saturday Waffles

Auntie T's Hawaiian Muffins

Aunt Toni's Blueberry Little Miss Muffins

Orange-Cranberry Scones

Grandaddy's Biscuits

Hash Browns and Cheese Casserole

Sweet Potato Cakes with Applesauce

Shrimp 'n' Grits

Egg-White Veggie Frittata

Leek and Bacon Quiche

Spinach, Red Pepper, and Goat Cheese Quiche

Girl Scout Camp French Toast

8 tablespoons (1 stick) unsalted butter, melted

1 cup packed brown sugar

2 large eggs

1½ cups whole milk

2 tablespoons freshly squeezed orange juice

1 teaspoon vanilla extract

½ teaspoon ground cinnamon

¼ teaspoon table salt

12 slices day-old brioche, challah, or French bread, sliced 1 inch thick

I learned how to make this recipe at Girl Scout camp when I was a kid. It's still the best French toast around! I insist on using a good-quality bread such as brioche, challah, or French. These loaves have excellent flavor on their own, and hold up well after being dipped in the custard mixture. Tony loves this French toast, in part because he's not a big maple syrup guy. Here, the brown sugar and butter make a sweet, sticky topping that's way better than syrup. **Makes 6 servings**

1. Preheat the oven to 375° F. Place the melted butter in a rimmed baking sheet or jelly-roll pan. Add the brown sugar and mix thoroughly until all the sugar has dissolved. Spread the mixture evenly in the pan.

2. In a pie plate or other shallow dish, lightly beat the eggs. Add the milk, orange juice, vanilla, cinnamon, and salt, and mix well. Dip both sides of the bread slices into the egg mixture, then transfer them to the baking sheet.

3. Bake until the bread is golden brown on top and the syrup on the bottom is bubbling, 20 to 25 minutes. To serve, use a spatula to flip the bread onto plates, sugar side up.

Light-as-a-Feather Pancakes

These pancakes really are feather-light. Tony loves them because he can eat a whole stack without feeling like a vulture. **Makes 12 pancakes**

1. In a large bowl, whisk together the flour, sugar, baking powder, baking soda, and salt.

2. In a medium bowl, whisk together the buttermilk, eggs, butter, and vanilla.

3. Make a well in the center of the dry ingredients. Pour in the buttermilk mixture and whisk until almost smooth (do not over-beat).

4. Heat a nonstick skillet or griddle over medium-high heat and spray with cooking spray or brush with melted butter. Spoon ⅓ cup of the batter onto the hot pan for each pancake, and cook until the top begins to bubble and the edges begin to brown, 3 to 4 minutes. Turn and cook until the second side is light golden, about 1 minute more. Transfer to a plate. Serve immediately with maple syrup and butter, or keep warm in a 200° F oven on a rack set over a baking sheet, adding pancakes as you go until the entire batch is cooked.

2 cups all-purpose flour

2 tablespoons sugar

1½ teaspoons baking powder

½ teaspoon baking soda

¼ teaspoon salt

2 cups low-fat buttermilk

2 large eggs, lightly beaten

2 tablespoons unsalted butter, melted

2 teaspoons vanilla extract

Cooking spray or melted butter

Maple syrup and butter

Whole Wheat Pancakes

1 cup whole wheat flour

1 cup all-purpose flour

1½ tablespoons sugar

1 teaspoon baking soda

1/4 teaspoon salt

1½ cups vanilla soy milk

1/2 cup nonfat yogurt

2 large egg whites

1 teaspoon vanilla extract

Cooking spray or melted butter

Maple syrup and fresh berries

These very healthful pancakes are also light and flavorful, but without all the fat. They are the kind of thing to serve for a weekend breakfast when you want something a little special, but not over the top. The berry smoothie is a good go-with, since it adds more protein and fruit to start your day.

Makes 12 pancakes

1. In a large bowl, combine the flours, sugar, baking soda, and salt.

2. In a medium bowl, whisk together the soy milk, yogurt, egg whites, and vanilla. Pour the wet ingredients into the flour mixture and whisk just until smooth (do not overbeat).

3. Heat a nonstick skillet or griddle over medium-high heat and spray with cooking spray or brush with melted butter. Spoon ⅓ cup of the batter onto the hot pan for each pancake, and cook until the top begins to bubble and the edges begin to brown, 2 to 3 minutes. Turn and cook until the second side is light golden, about 1 minute more. Transfer to plates and serve immediately with maple syrup and fresh berries.

Berry Smoothie

Makes 2 servings

2 frozen ripe bananas, cut into chunks

1 cup frozen strawberries

2 scoops vanilla-flavored whey protein powder

1 cup light soy milk

Freshly squeezed juice of 1/2 lime

In a blender, combine all the ingredients and blend until smooth. Serve immediately.

Chocolate Waffles

You can't go wrong when you add chocolate to anything, including breakfast. This is the kind of thing to serve someone for breakfast in bed on their birthday or on Valentine's Day. Or add whipped cream or ice cream and serve them for dessert. **Makes 4 to 6 servings**

1. In a large bowl, combine all of the ingredients except the cooking spray and strawberries and whisk until fluffy.

2. Preheat the waffle iron. Once the waffle iron reaches the desired temperature, spray it lightly with cooking spray or brush it with melted butter.

3. Spread a ladleful of batter onto the waffle iron and cook until the waffles are golden and set (the steam should have reduced significantly), 3 to 5 minutes.

4. Serve immediately with fresh strawberries on top, or, if not serving immediately, keep warm in a 200° F oven on a rack set over a baking sheet, adding waffles as you go until the entire batch is cooked. The waffles can also be cooled, then frozen in resealable plastic bags. To serve, reheat the frozen waffles in the toaster.

Note: Dutch Cocoa Powder Dutch cocoa powder (also called Dutch-process or alkalized unsweetened cocoa powder) is treated with an alkali that neutralizes its acids. The result is a delicate, subtle flavor, perfect for light chocolate pastries. High-quality Dutch cocoa powder, such as Valrhona and Lindt, can be purchased in most supermarket baking aisles or in specialty food markets.

2 cups all-purpose flour

1 3/4 cups buttermilk

8 tablespoons (1 stick) unsalted butter, melted

1/4 cup Dutch cocoa powder (see note)

1/4 cup sugar

2 large eggs

1 tablespoon baking powder

1 teaspoon vanilla extract

1/4 teaspoon salt

Cooking spray or melted butter

1 pint fresh strawberries, sliced

Uncle D's Saturday Waffles

2 cups all-purpose flour

1 3/4 cups buttermilk

8 tablespoons (1 stick) unsalted butter, melted

2 large eggs

1 1/2 tablespoons sugar

1 tablespoon baking powder

1 teaspoon vanilla extract

1/4 teaspoon salt

Cooking spray or melted butter

When I was growing up, nearly every week on Saturday mornings we used to go to my aunt Toni's house for brunch. My uncle Darryl always made his buttery waffles, served with bacon, sausage, omelets, and skillet potatoes for a killer meal. Now, I don't make waffles every weekend, but when I do, I go to this recipe. Tony is wild about them. **Makes 8 servings**

1. In a large bowl, whisk together all the ingredients except the cooking spray until fluffy.

2. Preheat the waffle iron. Once the waffle iron reaches the desired temperature, spray it lightly with cooking spray or brush it with melted butter.

3. Fill a medium-size ladle with batter and pour it onto the waffle iron. Cook until the waffle is golden brown and the steam has reduced significantly, 3 to 5 minutes.

Chocolate-Banana Smoothie

Makes 2 servings

2 frozen ripe bananas, cut into chunks

2 scoops chocolate-flavored whey protein powder

1 1/2 cups light soy milk

1 cup nonfat yogurt

1/2 cup smooth peanut butter

1/2 cup crushed ice

This is Tony's favorite shake to drink after a workout. The protein helps repair body tissue that is broken down during exercise, and both the peanut butter and bananas replenish energy that is lost during a vigorous workout. It also makes a waffle brunch a little more substantial in terms of nutrients.

In a blender, combine all the ingredients and blend until smooth. Serve immediately.

4. Serve immediately or place in a 200° F oven on a wire rack set over a rimmed baking sheet, adding waffles as you go until the entire batch is cooked. The waffles can also be cooled, then frozen in resealable plastic bags for up to 2 months. To serve, reheat the frozen waffles in the toaster.

✳ Auntie T's Hawaiian Muffins

Auntie T's blueberry muffins (page 158) are my favorite, but these slightly denser muffins, loaded with macadamia nuts, pineapple, and coconut, are Tony's. And he's half Hawaiian, so he loves that these are a nod to his heritage. They are exotic and superb. **Makes 10 muffins**

1. Preheat the oven to 400° F and spray 10 cups of a muffin tin with cooking spray (fill the remaining 2 cups with ½ inch of water).

2. In a bowl, sift or whisk together the flour, baking powder, and salt. Crumble in the brown sugar and whisk well.

3. In a small bowl, lightly beat the milk, pineapple and juice, coconut, butter, egg, and vanilla. Make a well in the center of the dry ingredients, pour in the wet ingredients, and stir until almost combined (avoid overmixing). Briefly fold in the nuts, and divide the batter among the muffin cups.

4. Bake 18 to 20 minutes, until a toothpick inserted into the center of a muffin comes out clean. Serve warm or let cool, then freeze in resealable plastic bags. (To reheat, halve the muffins crosswise horizontally and warm on a baking sheet in a 450° F oven for 5 minutes.)

Cooking spray

2 cups all-purpose flour

1½ teaspoons baking powder

¼ teaspoon salt

1 cup light brown sugar, packed

¾ cup whole milk

½ cup canned crushed pineapple, with juice

6 tablespoons sweetened coconut flakes

4 tablespoons (½ stick) unsalted butter, melted and cooled

1 large egg

½ teaspoon vanilla extract

½ cup chopped roasted macadamia nuts

Aunt Toni's Blueberry Little Miss Muffins

Cooking spray

2 cups all-purpose flour

1/4 cup plus 11/2 teaspoons sugar

11/2 teaspoons baking powder

1/4 teaspoon salt

1/2 cup whole milk

1/4 cup vegetable oil

1 large egg

1/2 teaspoon vanilla extract

3/4 cup blueberries, preferably fresh (thawed if frozen)

1/2 teaspoon finely grated lemon zest

For the streusel topping:

2 tablespoons cold unsalted butter, cubed

2 tablespoons all-purpose flour

2 tablespoons sugar

1/2 teaspoon finely grated lemon zest

My aunt Toni used to have a muffin business called Little Miss Muffin. She made more than fifty different kinds of muffins, and each one was better than the next. What I love about her muffins is that they're easy, fluffy, and divine. With its streusel topping and sweet berries, blueberry has always been my favorite. **Makes 10 muffins**

1. Preheat the oven to 400° F and spray 10 cups of a muffin tin with cooking spray (fill the remaining 2 cups with ½ inch of water).

2. In a large bowl, sift or whisk together the flour, ¼ cup of the sugar, the baking powder, and salt.

3. In another bowl, whisk together the milk, oil, egg, and vanilla.

4. In a small bowl, toss the blueberries with the lemon zest and the remaining 1½ teaspoons of sugar.

5. Make a well in the center of the dry ingredients, pour in the wet ingredients, and stir until almost combined (avoid overmixing). Briefly fold in the blueberries, and divide the batter among the muffin cups.

6. For the streusel topping, using your fingers or a pastry blender, work together the butter, flour, sugar, and lemon zest until the mixture resembles coarse crumbs. Sprinkle the streusel evenly over the muffins.

7. Bake 14 to 16 minutes, until a toothpick inserted into the center of a muffin comes out clean. Serve warm or let cool, then freeze in resealable plastic bags. (To reheat, halve the muffins crosswise horizontally and warm on a baking sheet in a 450° F oven for 5 minutes.)

✳ Orange-Cranberry Scones

These scones are delicious and very light, with a texture that's more like a biscuit than a scone. You can use any dried fruit in place of the cranberries—raisins are classic—but the cranberries do add a nice tart taste. **Makes 10 scones**

1. Preheat the oven to 450° F and line a large baking sheet with parchment paper.

2. In a large bowl, sift together the cake flour, 2 tablespoons of the sugar, the baking powder, and the salt. Using your fingers, work the butter into the flour mixture until the mixture resembles coarse crumbs.

3. In a small bowl, whisk together 2 of the eggs, the cream, and the vanilla.

4. Make a well in the center of the dry ingredients and pour in the cream mixture. Stir until just combined. Fold in the dried cranberries, walnuts, and orange zest, stirring 3 more times to incorporate.

5. Turn the dough onto a lightly floured surface and knead gently, about 6 times (no more than 10). The dough will be fairly sticky. If necessary, add extra flour, 1 tablespoon at a time (but avoid adding too much flour, or the scones will become heavy).

6. Pat the dough to ¾-inch thickness. Cut into triangles, reshape the leftover dough, and repeat. Place the scones on the prepared baking sheet.

7. Beat the remaining egg with 1 tablespoon of water and brush over the tops of the scones. Sprinkle the remaining sugar evenly over the scones. Bake 10 to 12 minutes, until golden brown. Serve warm.

2 cups cake flour, plus extra for kneading

3 tablespoons sugar

1 tablespoon baking powder

1/2 teaspoon salt

5 tablespoons cold unsalted butter, cut into pieces

3 large eggs

3/4 cup heavy cream

1 teaspoon vanilla extract

1/3 cup dried cranberries

1/3 cup chopped walnuts (preferably black walnuts)

Finely grated zest of 1 large orange

Grandaddy's Biscuits

2 cups all-purpose flour, plus extra for kneading

4 teaspoons baking powder

1/2 teaspoon salt

1/4 teaspoon baking soda

2 tablespoons cold butter, cut into pieces

2 tablespoons cold shortening, cut into pieces

1 cup cold buttermilk

Having brunch at my grandparents' house almost every Sunday was the highlight of my week when I was growing up. No Sunday brunch ever passed without my grandaddy's famous biscuits, which we ate hot with butter on top. I still make them at least twice a month, though I've changed the recipe slightly for a lighter version that is just as flaky and buttery as his was. **Makes 6 servings**

1. Preheat the oven to 450° F. Line a baking sheet with parchment paper.

2. In a large mixing bowl, sift together the flour, baking powder, salt, and baking soda. Using a pastry blender or two knives, cut the butter and shortening into the flour mixture until it resembles coarse crumbs.

3. Make a well in the center of the dry ingredients and add the buttermilk. Using a fork, stir the mixture until just combined (avoid overmixing).

4. Turn the dough onto a lightly floured surface and fold it over onto itself 5 times. Pat the dough into a disk about 1½ inches thick. Using a biscuit cutter or a glass, cut the dough to the desired size. Bake on the prepared baking sheet until golden brown, about 12 minutes.

✳ Hash Browns and Cheese Casserole

When we were in college, Tony and I used to have break-fast at a place that served a version of this decadent casserole, which is essentially a cross between hash brown potatoes and macaroni and cheese, served hot and bubbling from the oven. I prefer to buy hash browns from the refrigerator case, such as Simply Potatoes, which are readily available at most grocery stores. If you have to use frozen, thaw them in the refrigerator overnight. **Makes 8 servings**

1. Preheat the oven to 400° F. Lightly coat a baking dish with cooking spray and add the uncooked hash browns.

2. In a medium saucepan over medium-high heat, warm the oil. Add the onion, and cook, stirring, until softened, 3 to 5 minutes. Transfer the onion to the hash-brown mixture.

3. Reduce the heat to medium. Melt the butter in the pan, then whisk in the flour and cook, stirring constantly, for 4 minutes. Whisk in ½ cup of the milk until smooth. Gradually whisk in the remainder of the milk until smoothly combined (until no lumps remain). Add the salt and pepper, and cook, stirring, until the sauce coats the back of a spoon, about 5 minutes.

4. Take the pan off the heat and stir in the Cheddar and Monterey Jack cheeses. Taste and adjust the seasoning if necessary.

5. Pour the cheese sauce over the hash browns and stir to incorporate the sauce. Top with the Parmesan, and bake about 25 minutes, until brown and bubbly. Serve hot.

Cooking spray

1 pound prepared hash brown potatoes (such as Simply Potatoes or Cascadian Farm)

1 teaspoon extra virgin olive oil

1/4 cup finely chopped onion

4 tablespoons (1/2 stick) unsalted butter

1/4 cup all-purpose flour

2 1/2 cups low-fat milk

1 teaspoon kosher salt

1/2 teaspoon freshly ground black pepper

1 cup grated sharp Cheddar cheese

1/2 cup grated Monterey Jack cheese

1/4 cup grated Parmesan cheese

Sweet Potato Cakes with Applesauce

3 medium sweet potatoes, peeled and quartered

2 small shallots

1 large egg, beaten

2 tablespoons all-purpose flour

1/2 teaspoon kosher salt, plus additional

1/4 teaspoon baking powder

1/4 teaspoon freshly ground nutmeg

1 tablespoon unsalted butter

1 tablespoon canola oil

Freshly ground black pepper

Applesauce

Tony and I used to go to a Jewish restaurant/deli in Baltimore that had the best latkes. I wanted to make my own version of latkes at home, so I decided to use sweet potatoes, which have fewer calories than regular potatoes and are good for you, too. I serve them in the classic way, with applesauce. You can also add sour cream. **Makes 8 servings**

1. Preheat the oven to 225° F.

2. In the bowl of a food processor fitted with the finest grating attachment, grate the potatoes and shallots. (If you do not have a food processor, a box grater will also work.)

3. In a large bowl, combine the potatoes, shallots, and egg, and mix well. Add the flour, ½ teaspoon of salt, baking powder, and nutmeg, and stir until thoroughly combined.

4. In a large nonstick skillet over medium heat, warm the butter and oil. Drop heaping tablespoons of the potato mixture into the skillet, and cook until the cakes are golden brown on each side, 3 to 4 minutes. Transfer the cakes to a paper-towel-lined plate and season lightly with salt and pepper. Keep warm in the oven until all the cakes have been cooked. Serve warm, topped with applesauce.

✳ Shrimp 'n' Grits

When we lived in Baltimore we were regulars at a restaurant that specialized in Low Country cuisine. Tony ordered this dish one day and was hooked. The funny thing is he never liked grits until he had them smothered with shrimp and the spicy, oniony sauce. The shrimp sauce is also incredible served over poached eggs and biscuits—almost like a Creole eggs Benedict.

This is a great dish to serve when you're entertaining for brunch. You can make it a day in advance; just don't return the shrimp to the dish until the very last minute. That way you'll know they won't get overcooked. **Makes 4 to 6 servings**

1. In a large sauté pan over medium-high heat, brown the sausage on all sides, about 5 minutes. Use a slotted spoon to transfer the sausage to a plate. Add the shrimp and Cajun seasoning to the pan, and cook until the shrimp are barely cooked through, 2 to 3 minutes. Transfer to another plate.

2. Reduce the heat to medium and melt the butter in the pan. Whisk in the flour and cook, stirring constantly, until the roux is nut-brown and fragrant, about 3 minutes. Add the onions, bell peppers, and celery, and cook, stirring, until softened, 6 to 8 minutes. Add the garlic, cayenne, and bay leaves, and cook for 30 seconds more.

3. Stir in the chicken broth and 1½ cups of water and bring to a boil. Return the sausage to the pan and reduce the heat to medium-low. Simmer uncovered, stirring occasionally, until the sauce has thickened, 10 to 12 minutes.

4. Raise the heat to medium-high. Add the cream and cook, stirring occasionally, for 5 minutes. Return the shrimp to the pan, along

1 pound andouille sausage, diced (see note, page 47)

1½ pounds large shrimp, peeled and deveined, tails left on (see note, page 20)

1/4 teaspoon Cajun seasoning (see note, page 54)

3 tablespoons unsalted butter

3 tablespoons all-purpose flour

1 cup chopped onions

1/2 cup chopped red bell pepper

1/2 cup chopped green bell pepper

1/2 cup chopped celery

2 teaspoons minced garlic

1/8 teaspoon cayenne pepper, or to taste

2 whole bay leaves

1 cup low-sodium chicken broth or stock

1/4 cup heavy cream

1/4 cup thinly sliced scallions

1/4 cup finely chopped fresh flat-leaf parsley

Kosher salt

Cooked stone-ground grits (see box, page 164) or polenta (see box, page 115)

Stone-ground Grits

Makes 4 servings

2 tablespoons unsalted butter
Kosher salt to taste
1 cup stone-ground grits

In a large pot, bring 4 cups of water, the butter, and salt to a boil. Add the grits slowly, return to a boil, then reduce the heat to a simmer. Cook, stirring occasionally to keep the grits from sticking, until creamy, 25 to 30 minutes. Serve hot.

with the scallions, parsley, and salt to taste, and cook until the shrimp are just heated through, about 2 more minutes. Taste and adjust the seasoning if necessary. Discard the bay leaves. Serve with hot, buttered stone-ground grits or polenta.

Egg-White Veggie Frittata

2 tablespoons plus 1 teaspoon extra virgin olive oil
3/4 cup fresh baby spinach
1/4 cup thinly sliced red onion
1/4 cup finely chopped red bell pepper
1/4 cup finely chopped poblano pepper
1 teaspoon minced garlic
12 large egg whites (1 1/2 cups) (see note)
1 teaspoon kosher salt
1/2 teaspoon freshly ground black pepper
1/3 cup grated Monterey Jack cheese, Cheddar cheese, or a combination
1/4 cup chopped fresh cilantro

I'm not a big fan of eggs, but I love frittata. It's an open-faced Italian omelet with some kind of vegetable, meat, or cheese filling. You can fill it with whatever your heart desires; here I've gone Southwestern, with poblano peppers, cilantro, and Monterey Jack cheese. I also like to use all egg whites to keep the protein count high and the cholesterol low.

Makes 6 servings

1. Preheat the broiler to high. In a 10-inch ovenproof skillet, preferably nonstick, over medium-high heat, warm 1 teaspoon of the olive oil. Add the spinach and cook, tossing, until wilted, about 1 minute. Transfer the spinach to a bowl and press on it with a paper towel to absorb any liquid it gives off. Finely chop the spinach and return it to the bowl.

2. Still over medium-high heat, add 1 tablespoon of the oil to the pan and cook the onion, stirring, until it just begins to brown, about 2 minutes. Add the peppers and cook until they soften, about 3 more minutes. Add the garlic, cook for 30 seconds more, then transfer to the bowl with the chopped spinach.

3. Lightly beat the egg whites with the salt and pepper. Reduce the heat to medium and add the remaining tablespoon of oil. When the oil is hot, add the egg whites and let them cook for 1 minute without stirring. Use a spatula to move the cooked egg toward the center of the pan, and tilt the pan to bring the uncooked egg to the outside. Continue to cook without stirring until the bottom of the frittata has set, about 3 minutes.

4. Sprinkle the vegetables over the frittata and then sprinkle on the cheese. Place the skillet under the broiler for 1 to 2 minutes, until the cheese is melted and slightly browned. Garnish with the cilantro, cut the frittata into wedges, and serve immediately.

Note: Egg Whites Most grocery stores carry cartons of egg whites, which makes it extremely convenient to have them anytime, without the fuss of separating all those eggs.

Leek and Bacon Quiche

1 (9-inch) prepared pie crust, blind-baked and cooled (see note)

1/2 pound thick-sliced bacon, chopped

2 leeks, white and light green parts, chopped

1 teaspoon fresh thyme leaves

4 large eggs

1 1/2 cups whole milk

1/4 teaspoon kosher salt

1/4 teaspoon freshly ground black pepper

3/4 cup grated Monterey Jack cheese

3/4 cup grated sharp Cheddar cheese

Quiche is great for brunch because you can make it the day before and reheat it. This is a kicked up quiche Lorraine, with two kinds of cheese and plenty of bacon. During Tony's rookie year, I'd make several quiches at a time and freeze them. That way, he could enjoy them when I wasn't there.

Makes one 9-inch tart to serve 6

1. Place the pan with the cooked pie crust on a rimmed baking sheet. Preheat the oven to 375° F and position an oven rack in the center of the oven.

2. In a large skillet over medium-high heat, cook the bacon until crisp, 15 to 20 minutes. Transfer it to a paper-towel-lined plate to drain. Add the leeks to the skillet and sauté them in the bacon fat until soft, 5 to 7 minutes. Add the thyme and cook for 1 minute. Transfer the leek mixture to a strainer set over a bowl to drain the excess liquid and grease.

3. In a large bowl, beat the eggs. Stir in the milk, salt, and pepper. Fold in the bacon, the drained leek mixture, and both cheeses. Pour the mixture into the pie crust. Bake the quiche on the baking sheet about 40 minutes, until set. Let it cool for about 10 minutes before slicing.

Note: Blind Baking To blind bake a pie crust, roll it out and place it in the pan, crimp the edges, then line the crust with a sheet of aluminum foil. Fill the pie with pie weights or dried beans. Bake at 350° F 10 to 15 minutes, until lightly browned. Remove the foil and the beans and let the crust cool before filling it.

Spinach, Red Pepper, and Goat Cheese Quiche

Once you know how to make a quiche, varying the filling is easy; you can basically use whatever cheese and vegetables you're in the mood for. This recipe is chock-full of veggies and creamy goat cheese. It makes a great, not-too-heavy lunch if you serve it with a green salad and some fresh fruit.

Makes one 9-inch tart to serve 6

1 (9-inch) prepared pie crust, blind-baked and cooled (see note, page 166)

2 tablespoons extra virgin olive oil

2 teaspoons minced garlic

1 1/4 pounds fresh baby spinach (about 5 quarts)

1/2 cup chopped roasted, peeled, and seeded red pepper (see box, page 51)

4 large eggs

1 cup whole milk

1/2 teaspoon kosher salt

1/4 teaspoon freshly ground black pepper

1/3 cup grated Parmigiano-Reggiano cheese

1/3 cup (about 4 ounces) crumbled fresh goat cheese

1. Place the pie crust in its pan on a rimmed baking sheet. Preheat the oven to 375° F and position an oven rack in the center of the oven.

2. In a large skillet over medium-high heat, warm the oil. Add the garlic and cook, stirring, for 30 seconds. Add the spinach and pepper and cook, stirring, until the spinach is completely wilted, about 5 minutes.

3. Transfer the spinach mixture to a fine mesh sieve set over a bowl and press on it to extract as much liquid as possible.

4. In a large bowl, beat the eggs. Stir in the milk, salt, and pepper. Mix in the spinach mixture and both cheeses. Pour this mixture into the pie crust.

5. Bake the quiche on the baking sheet until the center is just set, about 40 minutes. Let it cool for 10 minutes before slicing. Serve warm or at room temperature.

Desserts

Mango Sorbet

3 large ripe mangoes

1/4 cup light corn syrup

1/4 cup sugar, preferably superfine

This dessert has so much intense mango flavor, it's like eating a frozen mango. The key is making sure to use perfectly ripe mangoes. If you don't have an ice cream maker, you can make this into a granita. Just prepare the mango puree, then freeze it according to the directions in the Strawberry Granita recipe (page 171). **Makes 4 servings**

1. Peel the mangoes and use a spoon to scrape the flesh from the skins. Scrape off as much of the flesh clinging to the seeds as possible. Place the mango flesh in the bowl of a food processor or blender and puree. Add the corn syrup and sugar and process until the sugar dissolves. Pour the puree into a bowl and refrigerate until cold, about 1 hour.

2. Pour the puree into an ice cream maker and process according to the manufacturer's instructions. Spoon the sorbet into a container, cover, and freeze until firm or up to 3 days.

Strawberry Granita

This is a perfect dessert for a hot summer night, and it doesn't require an ice cream maker. If the granita gets too firm and you have trouble scraping it out with a fork, transfer it to a food processor and pulse for a few seconds to break it up. Then serve it immediately, or refreeze it until needed.

Makes 4 servings

2 cups fresh or frozen strawberries

1/2 cup sugar, preferably superfine

1/4 cup Grand Marnier, or other orange liqueur

4 fresh strawberries

1. Using a food processor or blender, combine the 2 cups of strawberries, 1¼ cups of water, the sugar, and the Grand Marnier. Puree until smooth. Pour the puree through a sieve set over a metal bowl to remove the seeds. Press firmly, using a rubber spatula, to extract as much liquid as possible, and discard the solids.

2. Freeze the puree, whisking every 30 minutes, until somewhat firm, about 3 hours. Cover the puree and freeze without stirring until frozen solid, at least 2 hours longer and up to 3 days.

3. One hour before serving, place 4 cocktail glasses in the freezer.

4. To serve, use a fork to scrape the surface of the granita to form ice crystals. Scoop the crystals into the frozen glasses, garnish each with a fresh strawberry, and serve at once.

Vanilla-Bean Ice Cream

1 vanilla bean, halved lengthwise

3 cups half-and-half

3/4 cup sugar

6 egg yolks

2 teaspoons vanilla extract

When I was growing up, I remember my grandaddy sitting on the porch putting rock salt in the old-fashioned ice cream churner. For him, making ice cream was a labor of love. We would all wait around, salivating until it was ready. Back then it seemed like it took hours! Now I have a modern ice cream maker, so churning ice cream and sorbet is less of a special-occasion thing. But homemade ice cream like this one still makes me salivate. For something really decadent, add scoops of homemade vanilla ice cream to White Russian cocktails (see box). It's an outrageous adult dessert.

Makes 8 servings

1. Using the back of a knife, scrape the seeds inside the vanilla bean into a medium saucepan and then add the pod. Add the half-and-half and stir to combine. Bring the mixture to a simmer over high heat, then turn off the heat, cover, and steep for 15 minutes to infuse. Pull out the pod and discard or save for another purpose.

2. Whisk together the sugar and egg yolks until they are pale yellow and thick, about 2 minutes. Gradually pour the hot half-and-half into the egg mixture, whisking constantly. Return the mixture to the pan over medium-low heat, and cook at just below a simmer, stirring constantly with a wooden spoon, until the mixture coats the back of the spoon, about 5 minutes. Do not let it come to a boil.

3. Pour the custard through a sieve set over a bowl. Add the vanilla, and refrigerate until cold, about 1 hour. Transfer the custard to an ice cream maker and process according to the manufacturer's instructions. Transfer the ice cream to a container, cover, and freeze until firm or up to 3 days.

White Russian

Makes 4 servings

Fill 4 short glasses with ice. Pour 2 ounces of vodka, 1 ounce of Kahlúa, and 1 1/2 ounces of half-and-half into each glass. Stir until well-mixed. If you want to add scoops of ice cream, use a larger glass and skip the ice.

8 ounces premium vodka (such as Absolut)

4 ounces coffee-flavored liqueur (such as Kahlúa)

6 ounces half-and-half

Lemon Bars

E veryone loves lemon bars; they're tart, creamy, and yummy—like bite-size lemon meringue pies without the meringue, and easier to make. Case in point: I've been making these since I was twelve. **Makes 10 servings**

1. Preheat the oven to 350° F and grease an 8-inch square baking pan.

2. In the bowl of an electric mixer fitted with the paddle attachment, cream the butter and confectioners' sugar. Add the flour and mix until combined. Press the flour mixture into the bottom of the pan, going about ½ inch up the sides. Bake for 15 minutes, remove from the oven, and set aside.

3. In the clean bowl of an electric mixer fitted with the whisk attachment, beat the remaining ingredients until light and fluffy, about 3 minutes. Pour the mixture over the crust and bake about 25 minutes, until firm on the edges but still slightly soft in the center. Cool completely and cut into squares. Store covered in the refrigerator for up to 2 days.

8 tablespoons (1 stick) unsalted butter, softened, plus more for the pan

1/4 cup confectioners' sugar

1 cup all-purpose flour

2 large eggs

1 cup granulated sugar

2 tablespoons finely grated lemon zest

2 tablespoons freshly squeezed lemon juice

1 teaspoon vanilla extract

1/2 teaspoon baking powder

1/4 teaspoon kosher salt

Peanut Butter Bars

Cooking spray

3/4 cup smooth peanut butter

3/4 cup packed light brown sugar

1/2 cup granulated sugar

4 tablespoons (1/2 stick) unsalted butter, softened

1/4 cup shortening

1 large egg

3 tablespoons milk

1 tablespoon vanilla extract

1 1/4 cups all-purpose flour

3/4 teaspoon baking soda

1/2 teaspoon kosher salt

Given his love of anything made with peanut butter, these are Tony's favorite cookies. Cut into manly bars, they are easy and quick to make. **Makes about 24 bars**

1. Preheat the oven to 375° F. Grease a 13 x 9-inch pan with cooking spray.

2. Using an electric mixer, cream the peanut butter, both sugars, butter, and shortening until light and fluffy. Beat in the egg, milk, and vanilla.

3. In a small bowl, whisk together the flour, baking soda, and salt. Add the flour mixture to the wet ingredients and mix until combined.

4. Transfer the dough to the refrigerator and chill, covered, for 1 hour. (The dough can also be placed in a resealable plastic bag and frozen for up to 2 months. When you are ready to bake the bars, defrost the dough in the refrigerator until soft, 2 to 3 hours.)

5. Spread the dough evenly in the prepared pan. Bake until a toothpick inserted in the center of the pan comes out clean, about 20 minutes. Cool on a wire rack for 10 minutes. Cut into squares and serve.

✳ Baked Apple Dumplings

make this dessert late at night when my sweet tooth hollers, which is often. I almost always have apples around, especially Granny Smiths, which are Tony's favorite snacking apple. Then I can quickly put this together using whatever dough I have in the freezer, whether it's pie dough or puff pastry. It is a really cool presentation because it looks like a whole apple surrounded by a buttery, flaky dough, and it tastes like a cross between baked apples and apple pie. Yum! **Makes 2 to 4 servings**

1/4 cup packed light brown sugar

2 tablespoons unsalted butter or margarine, softened

1/4 teaspoon vanilla extract

1/4 teaspoon ground cinnamon

2 Granny Smith apples, peeled and cored

1 (17-ounce) package frozen puff-pastry dough, thawed

Vanilla-Bean Ice Cream (page 172) or whipped cream

1. Preheat the oven to 425° F. Line a baking sheet with parchment paper. In a small bowl, combine the brown sugar, butter, vanilla, and cinnamon, and mix well.

2. Cut the puff-pastry sheet in half (if the package comes with two sheets, use one sheet for each apple). On a lightly floured surface, roll out each pastry sheet until it is large enough to cover an entire apple. Using a sharp knife, make a 3-inch-long diagonal slit in each of the four corners of the pastry sheet.

3. Place an apple in the center of a pastry sheet and stuff the apple cavity with half of the brown-sugar mixture, spreading any filling that doesn't fit on the outside of the apple. Pull each corner of the puff pastry up over the apple, pinching the seams together to seal. Repeat with the remaining apple.

4. Place both apples on the prepared baking sheet. Bake for 10 minutes, then reduce the oven temperature to 350° F. Bake the apples about 40 minutes, until the pastry is golden brown and the apples are easily pierced with a fork. Cut each apple in half and place the halves pastry-side up on four plates. Serve with Vanilla-Bean Ice Cream or whipped cream.

Peach Crisp

For the filling:

1/4 cup granulated sugar

2 tablespoons cornstarch

1/4 teaspoon kosher salt

8 cups fresh peaches, peeled and quartered (about 2 1/2 pounds)

1 teaspoon vanilla extract

For the topping:

1 1/2 cups old-fashioned rolled oats

1/2 cup all-purpose flour

1 cup walnuts, finely chopped

1/2 cup packed light or dark brown sugar

1/4 teaspoon kosher salt

1/4 teaspoon ground cinnamon

8 tablespoons (1 stick) unsalted butter, melted

With their crumbly-crunchy nut toppings and sweet juicy layers of fruit, I just love crisps. I make them with whatever fruit is the freshest and ripest at the time, so feel free to substitute in this recipe—just adjust the amount of sugar in the filling if you are using a very sweet fruit, like blueberries, or if your fruit is very tart. Serve this with Vanilla-Bean Ice Cream (page 172) or whipped cream if you like.

Makes 6 servings

1. Preheat the oven to 375° F.

2. To make the filling, in a large bowl, stir together the sugar, cornstarch, and salt. Add the peaches and vanilla and toss to coat. Transfer the mixture to a 13 X 9-inch baking dish.

3. To make the topping, using a food processor, pulse the oats until they are coarsely ground, 5 to 10 seconds. In a medium bowl, combine the oats, flour, walnuts, brown sugar, salt, and cinnamon, and mix well. Stir in the melted butter until moistened. Sprinkle over the fruit.

4. Bake 40 to 50 minutes, until the topping is golden brown and the fruit is bubbly. Remove from the oven and let cool 20 minutes before serving.

Black-Bottom Banana Cream Pie

This is my take on Southern banana pudding. Instead of using vanilla wafers, I make this in a pie crust, and I increase the decadence factor by adding a layer of chocolate. Don't be tempted to use a crumb crust for this recipe; when you try to spread melted chocolate on the crumbs, they will stick to the spatula and not the crust.

One 9-inch pie to serve 8

1. Spread the bottom of the pie crust with the melted chocolate. Have the egg yolks ready in a bowl near the stove.

2. In a medium saucepan over medium heat, whisk together the milk, sugar, cornstarch, and salt. Cook, stirring, until the mixture is boiling and thick, 8 to 10 minutes.

3. Whisking constantly, pour some of the custard over the egg yolks. Continuing to whisk, add this yolk mixture back to the saucepan. Simmer the mixture over medium heat, stirring constantly, for 5 minutes. Transfer to a bowl and stir in the vanilla and crème de banana. Set aside until warm, not hot, 20 to 30 minutes.

4. Layer ⅓ of the banana slices on the bottom of the chocolate-lined pie crust. Pour ⅓ of the custard over the bananas. Repeat this layering twice more, ending with custard. Lay a piece of plastic over the pie and refrigerate for at least 4 hours and up to 3 days.

5. Before serving, use a vegetable peeler to shave thin curls of chocolate all over the top of the pie.

1 (9-inch) prepared pie crust, blind-baked and cooled (see note, page 166)

1/3 cup semisweet chocolate chips (or 2½ ounces semisweet chocolate), melted

4 large egg yolks, lightly beaten

2½ cups whole milk

3/4 cup sugar

1/4 cup cornstarch

1/8 teaspoon kosher salt

1 teaspoon vanilla extract

1 teaspoon crème de banana or dark rum

4 ripe yet firm bananas, sliced

1/2 ounce chocolate bar, for chocolate curls

Classic Cheesecake
with Strawberry-Mint Sauce

For the graham-cracker crust:

2 cups graham-cracker crumbs

1 cup pecans, finely ground

10 tablespoons unsalted butter, melted

1/4 cup sugar

For the cream-cheese filling:

4 (8-ounce) packages cream cheese, softened

1¼ cups sugar

4 eggs

2 teaspoons vanilla extract

Finely grated zest and juice of 1 lemon

1/4 cup all-purpose flour

1 cup sour cream

1/4 cup heavy cream

For the strawberry-mint sauce:

1 (10-ounce) package frozen sweetened strawberries, thawed

1 teaspoon freshly squeezed lemon juice

1 teaspoon vanilla extract

1 tablespoon fresh mint leaves, cut into a chiffonade (see note, page 32)

Together, my aunt Toni and I created what we consider to be the ultimate cheesecake recipe, but it took a lot of tries to get it right. The result is a classic New York–style cake with a dense, creamy filling that's not too heavy and has a nice lemony zing. I like to serve it with strawberry-mint sauce, but you can use sliced fresh strawberries if you'd rather. You need to make this the day before, so plan ahead. **Makes 10 servings**

1. Preheat the oven to 350° F. To make the crust, in a medium bowl, combine the graham-cracker crumbs, pecans, butter, and sugar, and mix well.

2. Using your hands, press the crust into the bottom and up the sides of a 10-inch springform pan. Using the bottom of a glass, press the bottom and the sides of the crust to distribute it evenly.

3. Transfer the crust, in the pan, to the freezer for 30 minutes to prevent it from sliding down the sides of the pan. Then bake 10 to 12 minutes, until lightly browned. Transfer the crust to a wire rack and cool completely. Reduce the oven temperature to 325° F.

4. To make the filling, in the bowl of an electric mixer fitted with the paddle attachment, beat the cream cheese until very fluffy. Add the sugar, eggs (one at a time), vanilla, and lemon zest and juice. Scrape the sides of the bowl and beat until smooth.

5. Sprinkle the flour on top of the filling and mix gently. Using a wooden spoon or a rubber spatula, fold in the sour cream and heavy cream until just combined. Pour the filling into the springform pan.

6. Bring a kettle of water to a boil. Set the pan on a wide sheet of heavy-duty aluminum foil (or use a double layer of regular foil), and fold the foil up the sides of the pan. Place the foil-wrapped pan in a large roasting pan or casserole dish and transfer it to the oven. Fill the roasting pan with about 1 inch of boiling water and bake about 1 hour, until the edges are set.

7. Turn off the oven and open the door slightly, and let the cake cool in the oven for 1 hour. Remove the cake from the oven and discard the foil. Transfer to a rack to cool to room temperature. Cover tightly with plastic wrap and refrigerate overnight.

8. To make the strawberry-mint sauce, using a food processor or a blender, combine the strawberries, lemon juice, and vanilla, and pulse until somewhat smooth. Transfer to a bowl, add the mint leaves, and stir to combine. Drizzle the sauce over slices of cheesecake and serve.

☀ Chocolate Soufflés

There is no dessert that says elegance like a soufflé. And there is certainly no dish out there more dramatic. Serving soufflés to your guests will make them feel like royalty as you present the hot, puffed chocolate confections pulled straight from the oven, but they are actually quite simple to make. The keys are beating tons of air into the egg whites and not overmixing the batter. Then it's no harder than baking muffins. Just don't tell your guests! **Makes 4 servings**

1. Bring the eggs to room temperature 30 minutes to 1 hour in advance. Preheat the oven to 350° F.

2. Coat four 1-cup ramekins with cooking spray or softened butter. Sprinkle the cups with sugar, and invert them to remove any excess sugar. Place the ramekins in a large casserole dish and set aside.

2 large eggs, separated, plus 2 egg whites

Cooking spray or softened butter

1/3 cup granulated sugar, plus more for dusting

1 cup milk

3 tablespoons unsalted butter

3 tablespoons all-purpose flour

2 ounces bittersweet chocolate

2 tablespoons Godiva liqueur (or other chocolate-flavored liqueur)

1 teaspoon vanilla extract

Pinch of fine sea salt

Confectioners' sugar

Fresh raspberries

3. In a small saucepan over low heat, bring the ⅓ cup sugar and milk to a simmer, stirring.

4. Meanwhile, in another small saucepan, melt the butter over medium-low heat. When the foam begins to subside, stir in the flour. Turn the heat to low and cook, stirring almost constantly, until the flour-butter mixture turns a light golden color, about 3 minutes.

5. Slowly whisk in the hot milk. It will be quite thick. Stir in the chocolate and remove from the heat. Let cool for 5 minutes.

6. Beat the egg yolks into the chocolate mixture. Add the liqueur and the vanilla. (The recipe can be prepared a few hours in advance up to this point. Cool, cover, and refrigerate.)

7. Bring a kettle of water to a boil. In a stainless-steel bowl, beat the egg whites with the salt until just stiff. Stir a heaping spoonful of egg whites into the chocolate mixture to lighten it. Using a rubber spatula, fold in the remaining whites.

8. Fill the soufflé dishes with the batter and pour boiling water almost halfway up the sides of the casserole dish. Place the dish in the center of the oven and cook until puffed, 15 to 20 minutes. Dust with confectioners' sugar and serve immediately with fresh raspberries.

Bread Pudding
with Bourbon-Caramel Sauce

Tony is not a huge dessert person, but when he does crave something sweet, it's always bread pudding. This bread pudding recipe is light and very puddinglike, not at all dense and heavy, like some. I generally keep it classic but use bourbon for the caramel sauce, which some say is the best part.

Makes 8 servings

1. Preheat the oven to 350° F.

2. To make the bread mixture, in a large bowl, combine the milk, brown sugar, orange juice, orange zest, and cinnamon, and mix well. Add the bread and let stand until the liquid is absorbed, about 5 minutes.

3. To make the custard, in a large bowl, whisk together the eggs, buttermilk, brown sugar, bourbon, vanilla, and salt, and set aside.

4. Butter a large baking dish. Loosely spoon the bread mixture into the dish. Pour the custard over the bread mixture, and sprinkle with the granulated sugar. Bake about 50 minutes, until light golden and a toothpick inserted into the center comes out clean.

5. For the bourbon-caramel sauce, melt the butter in a small saucepan over medium heat. Whisk the brown sugar into the butter and cook until the sugar melts, stirring constantly, 3 to 5 minutes. Reduce the heat to low, stir in the cream, bourbon, vanilla, and salt, and bring to a simmer. (The sauce can be made up to 1 day ahead and stored, covered, in the refrigerator. To reheat, warm gently over low heat, adding 1 tablespoon of cream if it seems too thick.) Drizzle, warm, over slices of bread pudding and serve.

For the bread mixture:

2 1/2 cups whole milk

1/2 cup packed light brown sugar

2 tablespoons freshly squeezed orange juice

Finely grated zest of 1 orange

1 teaspoon ground cinnamon

6 cups high-quality bread (such as challah or French), cut into 2-inch cubes

For the custard:

2 eggs (at room temperature)

2 cups buttermilk

1/2 cup packed light brown sugar

1 tablespoon bourbon

2 teaspoons vanilla extract

1/4 teaspoon kosher salt

2 teaspoons granulated sugar

For the bourbon-caramel sauce:

2 tablespoons unsalted butter

1/2 cup packed light brown sugar

1 cup heavy whipping cream

1 tablespoon bourbon

1 teaspoon vanilla extract

Pinch of kosher salt

Vanilla-Bean
Crème Brûlée

1 vanilla bean, split
   lengthwise

1 1/2 cups heavy cream

1 cup whole milk

6 large egg yolks

1/2 cup granulated sugar

1 teaspoon vanilla extract

1/4 cup packed light brown
   sugar

Crème brûlée is a silky-smooth vanilla custard topped with a crunchy caramelized brown-sugar topping. It's always been a favorite of mine to order in restaurants, and recently I discovered that it's not at all hard to make at home. Make sure to use the vanilla bean. It adds an intense, unbeatable flavor that I think is part of what makes crème brûlée so compelling. You need to start this the day before you want to serve it, so plan ahead. Some people serve it warm or at room temperature, but Tony prefers it cold. **Makes 6 servings**

1. Preheat the oven to 350° F. Place six ¾-cup ramekins or custard cups in a roasting pan and set aside.

2. Using the back of a knife, scrape the seeds inside the vanilla bean into a medium saucepan and then add the pod. Add the cream and milk and stir to combine. Bring the cream mixture to a simmer and immediately turn off the heat. Cover and steep for 15 minutes to infuse. Pull out the vanilla pod and discard or save for another purpose.

3. In a large bowl, whisk together the egg yolks and sugar until they are pale yellow and thick. Gradually whisk the cream mixture into the yolk mixture, whisking constantly to form a smooth custard base. Add the vanilla and stir.

4. Divide the custard evenly among the ramekins. Pour enough very hot tap water into the roasting pan to come almost halfway up the sides of the ramekins. Bake 30 to 35 minutes, until the mixture just sets but jiggles slightly in the center.

5. Carefully remove the ramekins from the pan and place on a rack to cool to room temperature. Cover them with plastic and chill overnight.

6. Place a rack as close to the broiler as possible. Sprinkle the top of each custard evenly with the brown sugar. Broil 1 to 2 minutes, until the sugar browns, watching very closely and turning the ramekins to brown them evenly.

7. Refrigerate until the custards are firm again but the topping is still crisp, 1 to 2 hours.

Index

Buffalo chicken tenders, 17
Butter
    lemon-shallot, whole trout en papillote
        with, 86–87
    Old Bay, roasted corn with, 141

C

Cabbage
    Asian steak salad with spicy vinaigrette,
        36–37
    Mom's stuffed cabbage, 108
    "pickled" red cabbage, 139
Cabrales, beef Wellington with, 122–23
Caesar chicken wrap, 61
Caesar salad with rustic croutons, 27
Cajun seafood pasta, 71
Cajun-style king crab legs, 92–93
Capers
    chicken with olives, sun-dried tomatoes,
        and, 97
    linguine alla puttanesca, 69
    quick chicken piccata, 96
Caramel
    bourbon-caramel sauce, bread pudding
        with, 181
Casserole, hash browns and cheese, 161
Catfish, blackened, 87
Caviar, crispy dilled potato cakes with,
    18–19
Cheese. *See also specific types*
    BBQ chicken pizza with Cheddar and
        Monterey Jack, 58
    chicken Parmesan, 98–99
    chicken quesadillas with mango, 16
    egg-white veggie frittata, 164–65
    five-cheese pizza with sun-dried tomato
        sauce, 59
    garlic cheese bread, spaghetti and
        meatballs with, 74–75
    hash browns and cheese casserole, 161
    herbed turkey cheese burger with bacon
        and chipotle mayo, 63
    leek and bacon quiche, 166
    Reuben melt, 62

spinach, red pepper, and goat cheese
    quiche, 167
two-potato gratin, 145
Cheesecake, classic, with strawberry-mint
    sauce, 178–79
Cherry port sauce, seared duck breasts with,
    103
Chicken
    Aunt Laura's teriyaki wings, 15
    BBQ chicken pizza with Cheddar and
        Monterey Jack, 58
    buffalo chicken tenders, 17
    chicken Caesar wrap, 61
    chicken chili with roasted peppers,
        50–51
    chicken Parmesan, 98–99
    cornbread-stuffed chicken roulade, 99
    everyday curried chicken salad, 33
    Gran's get-well chicken soup, 42
    Jamaican jerk chicken wings, 14
    jambalaya, 46–47
    Levon's coastal curry chicken, 100
    Mom's fried chicken, 101–2
    with olives, capers, and sun-dried
        tomatoes, 97
    pad Thai, 77
    quesadillas, with mango, 16
    quick chicken piccata, 96
    Southwest chicken salad with chipotle
        dressing, 34–35
    ultimate chile relleno with three sauces,
        106–7
Chickpeas
    creamy hummus, 10
Chile(s). *See also* Chili; Chipotle; Salsa; Spicy
    dishes
    roasted chile sauce, 106–7
    spice-rubbed T-bone, 119
    ultimate chile relleno with three sauces,
        106–7
Chili
    chicken, with roasted peppers, 50–51
    Ma Duke's, 52
Chili-garlic dipping sauce, spinach salmon
    spring rolls with, 22–23

Mediterranean panini with prosciutto and
tapenade, 66
Mint
sauce, herb-and-garlic-crusted rack of
lamb with, 131
strawberry-mint sauce, classic cheesecake
with, 178-79
Mom's fried chicken, 101–2
Mom's stuffed cabbage, 108
Mozzarella
five-cheese pizza with sun-dried tomato
sauce, 59
Mediterranean panini with prosciutto and
tapenade, 66
tomato, mozzarella, and basil salad, 29
Muffins
Aunt Toni's blueberry Little Miss Muffins,
158
Hawaiian, Auntie T's, 157
Mushrooms
beef Wellington with Cabrales, 122–23
filet with sautéed mushrooms and onions,
121
Gran's beef stroganoff, 113–14
Mediterranean panini with prosciutto and
tapenade, 66
veal Marsala with, 129
veggie pizza, 56–57
warm spinach salad with bacon dressing, 30
wild mushroom risotto, 79

N

Noodles. *See also* Pasta
Gran's beef stroganoff, 113–14
Gran's get-well chicken soup, 42
homey braised short ribs over, 112
pad Thai, 77
soba noodles with five-spice flank steak,
78–79

O

Old Bay butter, roasted corn with, 141
Olives

chicken with capers, sun-dried tomatoes,
and, 97
linguine alla puttanesca, 69
Mediterranean panini with prosciutto and
tapenade, 66
Onions
filet with sautéed mushrooms and onions,
121
French onion soup, 41
veggie pizza, 56–57
Orange
orange cranberry scones, 159
orange-peel beef, 117
Osso buco with gremolata, 114–15

P

Pad Thai, 77
Pancakes
light-as-a-feather, 153
whole wheat, 154
Panini, Mediterranean, with prosciutto and
tapenade, 66
Panko-crusted pork chops, 126
Parmesan
chicken Parmesan, 98–99
Parsley
chimichurri sauce, churrasco con, 118
gremolata, osso buco with, 114–15
Pasta, 68–76
black, with creamy tomato and shrimp
sauce, 70
Cajun seafood pasta, 71
chicken Parmesan with, 98–99
linguine alla puttanesca, 69
linguine with fresh tomatoes and clams,
72
meat lovers' lasagna, 76
pasta pomodoro, 68
quick chicken piccata with, 96
seafood lasagna, 73
spaghetti and meatballs, 74–75
veal Marsala with mushrooms over, 129
veal scaloppine over, 128
Pasta salad with goat cheese, 32

Ma Duke's chili, 52
roasted tomato bisque with Brie toasts, 43
shrimp bisque, 44
smoked duck gumbo, 53–54
spicy Latin fish stew, 49
split pea soup with crispy prosciutto, 40
Szechuan beef 'n' veggies, 116
Southwest chicken salad with chipotle
  dressing, 34–35
Soy
  Asian salmon with ginger and, 88
  halibut with spicy soy broth, 85
Spaghetti
  and meatballs, 74–75
  pasta pomodoro, 68
Spiced basmati rice pilaf, 147
Spicy dishes. *See also* Chile(s); Chili;
  Chipotle; Salsa
  blackened catfish, 87
  Jamaican jerk chicken wings, 14
  perfect spicy guacamole, 8
  spice-rubbed T-bone, 119
  spicy cranberry sauce, Tex-Mex venison
    with, 134
  spicy Latin fish stew, 49
  spicy soy broth, halibut with, 85
  spicy vinaigrette, Asian steak salad with,
    36–37
Spinach
  egg-white veggie frittata, 164–65
  hot artichoke spinach dip, 12
  salad, warm, with bacon dressing, 30
  sautéed spinach with garlic, 136
  spinach, red pepper, and goat cheese
    quiche, 167
  spinach salmon spring rolls, 22–23
  turkey club and avocado wrap, 60
  veggie pizza, 56–57
Split pea soup with crispy prosciutto, 40
Squid-ink pasta with creamy tomato and
  shrimp sauce, 70
Steak. *See* Beef
Stews. See Soups and stews
Stone-ground grits, 164

Strawberries
  berry smoothie, 154
  fresh fruit salad, 26
  Gran's punch, 92
  lava flow, 15
  strawberry daiquiri, 83
  strawberry granita, 171
  strawberry lemonade, 102
  strawberry-mint sauce, classic cheesecake
    with, 178–79
Stuffed cabbage, Mom's, 108
Sugar snap pea and asparagus risotto, 80
Sun-dried tomato(es)
  chicken with olives, capers, and, 97
  sauce, five-cheese pizza with, 59
Sweet potatoes
  Levon's coastal curry chicken, 100
  mashed, 143
  sweet potato cakes with applesauce, 162
  two-potato gratin, 145
Swiss chard, sautéed, with balsamic vinegar,
  140
Szechuan beef 'n' veggies, 116

T

Tacos, fish, with mango salsa, 65
Tahini
  creamy hummus, 10
Tapenade, Mediterranean panini with
  prosciutto and, 66
Teriyaki wings, Aunt Laura's, 15
Tex-Mex venison with spicy cranberry sauce,
  134
Thyme and rosemary, seared veal chops with,
  127
Tomato(es)
  black pasta with creamy tomato and
    shrimp sauce, 70
  linguine alla puttanesca, 69
  linguine with fresh tomatoes and clams,
    72
  marinara sauce, 74, 98
  pasta pomodoro, 68